As the Twig is Bent

The Story of the Children's Country School

Paul DiMarco

First published by Dog Ear Publishing
4010 W. 86th Street, Ste H
Indianapolis, IN 46268
www.dogearpublishing.net

ISBN: 978-1-4575-0872-1

This book is printed on acid-free paper.

Printed in the United States of America

ACKNOWLEDGEMENTS

THANK YOU to Teré Aceves, Rick Bradley, John Brady, Firman Brown, Paul Busher, Vervaleen Trogden Burns, Jacqueline Christensen, Robin Clements, Dean Eyre, Elizabeth Boge Flehr, Jean Bradburn Galli, Barbara Hansen Harkness, Gerry Kanter, Roy Kimmel, Ernest Kraule, Felice Leeds, Marilyn Mitchell Lindquist, Francia Los Cimientos, Marjorie Junod Lubbes, Peter Maule, Dale McElroy, Lewis McLaren, Elizabeth Burke Merriman, Jacqueline Myatt Milikien, Liz Mitchell, Tom Mitchell, Barbara Morgan, Peggy Walsh Morse, Betty Timby O'Neill, Mary Keith Osborn, Nancy Haggerty Rudderman, Mark Silver, Isabel Gatley Starn, Sharon Shaefer Tedford, Marilyn Manson Towle, Pat Trogden, Jane Waggner, Jack Watkins, Tom Watts, Josephine West, Mariquita West, Irving Yabroff, Lou Yabroff,

SPECIAL THANK YOU to Masako Ishida "Miss Saki", Marion Martin, Bob Thompson, and Clare Wendy Yabroff for their insight into the personalities of the Four Founders of TCCS.

Jan Hill Boone, Richerd Cancilla, Bryan Epps, Warren Heid, Bob Klang, Tom Watkins, Tom Watts, and Bill Yabroff for their personal interviews and memorabilia including photographs, film, and artifacts from TCCS.

This book is dedicated to Mary Orem and the children of
The Children's Country School

PREFACE

He sat with legs crossed on a single planked wooden bench with a self-assured exuberant smile that hinted at something great. At his back was a storybook-styled house. His friend beside him leaned on a shovel as a make-shift cane. Both were dressed in corduroy; one in a jacket and the other in pants. They had non-descript haircuts that painted a post-Depression era. These boys were not affluent, but their demeanor offered a deeper riches. I was taken by the charming scene.

This photograph would begin a ten year search and rescue mission for a school history connected to the boy, his friend, and the storybook house. Inquiries into the written history of the school were met with collective fingers pointing to the old water tower on campus whose proximity nearly shadowed the little Dutch house in the photograph.

In September of 2002, I climbed the rickety stairs to the top of this 1918 tank house. I entered a room filled with metal file cabinets, boxes of forgotten folders, and other paperwork from the school's past business affairs. Searching through file cabinets, the oldest dated paper read 1981.

With no real expectations, I began to head for the door and down the stairs. I looked one last time across the room strewn with discarded items. In the corner, underneath three precariously stacked boxes of files, I saw a dark green rectangular box. The box looked out of place amongst the other objects in the room. I removed the boxes on top and pulled out the heavy green cardboard box which revealed itself to be a file cabinet that measured about 3 ft in length. I pulled on the front handle opening a cabinet filled to the brim with files. I arbitrarily pulled one file out in the middle and the date of the typed letter inside read 1938.

I would spend the next couple of months performing a routine that became the highlight of my days. At night, I would take a handful of files and read their contents in full. Most of the files included a tab with a student's last and first name. It was a treasure trove of papers dating back over 60 years, including letters from parents to the school, as well as letters from the school to the parents on ornate letter-head. Order forms for uniforms to Kladeze, receipts for tuition payments, and photographs of children from an era long passed were nestled neatly inside these files.

The most telling and intriguing part of these papers were the personal letters written in correspondence. Administrators were not writing to parents about their child's academic standing, but rather their social well-being and general disposition at the school. It soon became apparent that this Silicon Valley school of today was once a thriving country-infused boarding school of the 1930's. The more I read, the more I wanted to know. Who were Peaches, Helen of Troy, and Misty? What was the Pied Piper's Call? Where was the Village of Friendly Relations?

I wondered about these children whose once anonymous names now donned literary personalities. These children would now be adults in their late 60's and early 70's. My new mission was to find just one of these long ago students and have them tell me about this place of mystery and intrigue.

I began my search by using Yahoo people search. I would type in a name and the search engine would spit out all of the people with the same first and last names living in the United States. I would narrow my search to approximate age, and for the more common last names, I would restrict the search to California only.

I began the arduous, but exciting task of making blind phone calls (on the school's dime) across the United States. My message was generally this: Hi, my name is Paul DiMarco and I am calling from Los Gatos, California. I am wondering if you ever attended The Children's Country School? The answers varied, but most commonly I heard, "*I've never been to California*" or "*The Children's what?*"

Numerous phone calls were made to no avail. The more phone calls that I made, the more I expected the usual outcome of explaining the purpose of my phone call in more detail to the confused recipient or apologizing for disturbing an easily agitated stranger.

The first time I heard the answer of "*Yes*" come from one of my anonymous calls, the once closed door squeaked open. The first student was found living only a couple hours drive away in Napa, CA. She was a 1939 graduate of the school and gave me the name of two more students living in the Bay Area.

The more people I called, the more names I was given to find. In a year, I had found over 20 students. In two years, the number of students swelled to 35. My summers were spent interviewing these former students in person, on camera, or by phone. I was given photographs, memorabilia, a precious 1938 home movie of the campus, and story after story revealing the personality of this bustling boarding school.

I found the first student who entered the school at 17 months old. I spoke to one of the four graduates from the first graduating class of 1939 and most of the eight member graduating class of 1946. The only known adults alive from that era, a niece of the original founder and the school's horse back riding instructor were found.

Two significant finds were Bill Yabroff and a woman named Miss Saki. Bill Yabroff was the son of one of the founders of the school. Bill was the boy in the photograph sitting on the wooden bench. Through Bill, I was able to learn in detail the origin and growing pains of the country school. Bill came to campus and put names to children and adults in endless photographs. We walked the campus and he pointed out landmarks as I clung to his every syllable. Bill was able to verify what I had assumed: The Children's Country School was a story that needed to be told.

Miss Saki was a name mentioned numerous times by former students. They asked if I had found her. They said that she was a teacher at the school and had been in Los Gatos just a year or two earlier. If alive, she would be over 90 years old. Her given name was Masako Ishida.

I found three possible addresses in California for her: Campbell, Sacramento, and San Francisco. I wrote letters to no avail. I knocked on the door at the Campbell address with no luck. Months passed, and then one evening, the red light on my answering machine was blinking when I came in the door. The voice on the other end was old and withered exclaiming simply this is Miss Saki. She left no return phone number. Excited, yet exasperated, all I could do was wait. A few days passed, and then I heard the same voice when I picked up the receiver on a Saturday afternoon. I exclaimed, *"Miss Saki, I found you!"*...."*Yes,*" she replied, *"this is Miss Saki."*

Fondly known as Miss Saki by adults and children, she was hunched over and slow moving at 94. We met at her retirement home outside Sacramento where we sat and talked about her life at TCCS. She enthusiastically thumbed through large photo albums putting a name to every child's face from six decades past. For hours, we chatted about the early days of the school; the hardships; the perseverance; her love of the children; and especially, her love of teaching which was most evident in her voice.

A warm, sharp, insightful woman, Saki kept an envelope on her lap throughout our visit. The letter inside was written and signed by the four founders of The Children's Country School. The letter affectionately and deliberately declared her a silent partner to the founders, and therefore, the fifth founder.

It was the start of a friendship that included random phone calls by her, usually close to 10pm, in which she would tell me yet another story about the boarding school. Every conversation would end with an abrupt, *"OK then, good-night."* Miss Saki passed away in 2008.

By 2008, 60 members of the boarding school were found. As thrilled as some of them were to be able to tell their stories, I felt just as fortunate to be able to hear them. From 1935-1947, The Children's Country School would have more ups and downs than the stock market crash that preceded it or the infamous racehorse Seabiscuit during it.

And it all started from a simple idea: As the twig is bent, the tree will grow.

The
CHILDREN'S COUNTRY
SCHOOL
Day and Boarding

The
CHILDREN'S COUNTRY
SCHOOL
LOS GATOS · CALIFORNIA

CHAPTER 1

THE BIRTH OF AN IDEA

"It is not easy to be a pioneer - but oh, it is fascinating! I would not trade one moment, even the worst moment, for all the riches in the world."

~Elizabeth Blackwell[1]

As the twig is bent, the tree will grow. The Roman poet, Virgil, implies that things that affect and influence us in our childhood shape the kind of adult that we become. As a child's nature is shaped or bent, then his or her character will grow. This belief would be the mantra for The Children's Country School and its founder Mary Orem.

The second youngest of eleven siblings, Mary was born in 1892, the daughter of A.J. Orem, an educator, pioneer, and mining/railroad magnate.[2] Her Scottish ancestry can be traced back to the Mayflower, the original Pilgrim ship of 1620. All of her forefathers came to America prior to the Revolution.[3] The city of Orem, UT was named for Mary's brother, Walter, who was president of his father's conglomerate. The town was appreciative of the railroad stopping in their town en route from Provo and Salt Lake City.[4]

Mary was no stranger to adversity. Her ability to adapt was apparent at a young age as a mid-wife for her older sister, Mattie, when Mary was only 12 years old. In the late 1920's, her father lost his railroad and mining fortune over repayment of stockholders when outside mismanagement caused his company to fail. She took it upon herself the responsibility of earning a living for her elderly parents. She obtained a job with the newspaper as a reporter, and then, special columns writer. The apartment where she lived had rooms to share. Several young M.I.T. students were invited as paying guests. Confidence and resolve would become her strength.

She attended Wheelock Kindergarten College in Boston, Massachusetts. Two primary principles had been instilled into her thinking; training for peace begins in the nursery, and never leave a child whose eyes are still troubled. After graduating from Wheelock, Mary's progressive thinking brought her to work with Dr. Alfred Adler, the father of individual psychotherapy.

Mary Orem

In the early 1930's, Adler left Austria after his clinics there were closed due to his Jewish heritage. This happened despite the fact that he had converted to Christianity. He came to the United States for a professorship at the Long Island College of Medicine.[5] It was at this time that Mary became associated with Adler. She would spend weeks at a time in the homes of families studying and recording family dynamics. Mary would then report her findings.

Adler promoted social interest, belonging, and a need to eliminate pampering, neglect, and corporal punishment of children. He encouraged a democratic family structure for raising children. He recognized the need for developing an interest in the welfare of others, as well as a respect for nature. Even Adler's promotion of feminism on the heels of the women's suffrage movement appealed to Mary. Adler's ideas would have a significant effect on Mary's own thoughts on education.

She began to formulate her ideas for the perfect school, a place where environment and loving guidance would combine to help an individual develop to his or her fullest potential. In short, Mary wanted to test and establish the theory that environment raises the child, rather than genetics. With Social Darwinism's "survival of the fittest" prevalent in the world and close to reaching its darkest realization with the "superior race" mentality in Hitler's Germany, Mary was about to put into practice the idea of nurture over nature.

Elizabeth Glassford

Elizabeth Glassford was a former competitive swimmer and avid photographer. Elizabeth and Mary met in the late 1920's in Elizabeth's home state of New York. She was six years Mary's senior with a care-free nature about her that complimented Mary's driven focus. She was tall and athletic to Mary's short and stout. Always in pants and fond of Pendleton jackets, Elizabeth had a purpose to her walk. Both women shared progressive ideals. Elizabeth was at a crossroads in her life and ready to partake in a new venture.

Mary was at a crossroads herself. A year earlier, while in Chicago, her fiancé, Howard, had been fatally struck down as a pedestrian by a passing car. With both women ready to begin again, they became partners in starting a nursery school in nearby Nyack, NY.

In 1933, 1 in 3 Americans were out of work, and 2.2 million children were out of school. Some 24,000 schools would close across the country.[6] The Great Depression had a strangle hold on the nation and especially the East Coast. Mary and Elizabeth's nursery school would open and close in the same year.

News from the West Coast would bring more loss. A Western Union telegram from California sent word that Mary's older sister, Mattie, unexpectedly passed away in San Jose, CA. Mattie's husband owned a 10 acre fruit ranch in the neighboring city of Saratoga. There was a small two bedroom cottage located on the ranch. With no promising prospects in New York, the cottage in California became an intriguing destination.

Mary and Elizabeth decided to head West. With $100 between them, they loaded up a Model-T with two German shepherds, Hans and Gretel, and headed to California with dreams of a promising future.

Mary and Elizabeth set out on their trip across country. As they entered Illinois, their auto was desperately in need of repair. Mary had some connections at Hull House in Chicago and was able to find work there, while Elizabeth worked as a freelance photographer.

Jane Addams founded Hull House in 1897.[7] She was a prominent reformer of the Progressive Era and helped turn the nation to issues of concerns such as the needs of children and world peace. In 1931, she became the first woman to win a Nobel Peace Prize. At its height, Hull House was visited by over 2000 people a week. Its facilities included kindergarten classes, clubs for older students, a public kitchen, art gallery, coffeehouse, gym, a girl's club, book bindery, spa, music school, drama group, and library.[8]

As in her workings with Alfred Adler, Mary would gain inspiration from involvement with the Hull House. Addam's three primary ethical principles of teaching by example, cooperation, and social democracy would become central themes in Mary's future educational offerings.[9]

In the fall of 1933, Mary and Elizabeth arrived in California. Mary writes, "*Dearest Mae, Elizabeth and I arrived in San Jose on November eighth, 1933, in a Plymouth sedan filled to bursting with camera equipment, cases carrying most of our worldly goods. We had a brother-in-law's tiny cottage in his ten acre fruit ranch for the winter and one hundred dollars between us in our pockets. When I came to after Mattie's death followed so shortly by Dad's, I looked ten years older.*"

The freelance photography work produced little in means of pay. From Illinois came driblets instead of full payments and the driblets were sopped up by light, gas, and water bills. The nation was still in the grips of the Great Depression which would see the ladies' largest debtor from Illinois commit suicide.

Mary writes, "*The hundred dollars didn't last long. To avert hungry days, we sold our jewelry- even my mother's watch and sister's sorority pin. I don't know what would have happened if the Probation Officer (Mrs. McDonald, a friend of Mattie) had not asked us to take care of a little three year old ward of hers. For this, we were to receive the munificent fee of twenty five dollars a month.*

In April, came two little girls, ages respectively seventeen months and three years, whose father was out of work and whose mother had turned to previous training in Social Services in order to support the family. Next, two children, ages seventeen months and four years, tumbled into our three room, plus attic and porch, cottage. May brought a nineteen month baby who had never been out of a hospital bed.

In June, arrived seventeen month old, Smiley. Out of the seven, only the Bartletts come from the class of the 100% children. The other five are bits of flotsam and jetsam cast upon a storm-ridden shore of life— waif material. But, they have all the charm of happy childhood, laughing, romping, shining, babyhood.

We washed, ironed, bathed, powdered, cooked, housebroke, nose-wiped, swept floors, and made beds, built accredited playground equipment, laid a cement court and ran a first class Nursery School for our seven young charges."

Richerd Cancilla recalls, "*I was the first child of The Children's Country School. It was my home from a very small boy. I didn't grow up with my mother. I was taken away when I was very little, so I looked to Mary Orem as a substitute for my mother. I seldom even saw my mother only once or twice a year.*"

Original five nursery school children

November would bring two more children to the school and Christmas 1934 would bring a broken septic tank. Mary and Elizabeth had become the old woman who lived in a shoe busting at the seams.

Their nursery school had become a public spectacle. Automobiles would slow down as they passed the house of young children in the front yard doing tumbling gymnastics, painting on large easels, and practicing music on rudimentary instruments. This was not your ordinary nursery school of the day. It was around this time that the ladies caught the attention of two prominent figures in the area, Senator Sanborn Young and his wife, author Ruth Comfort Mitchell.

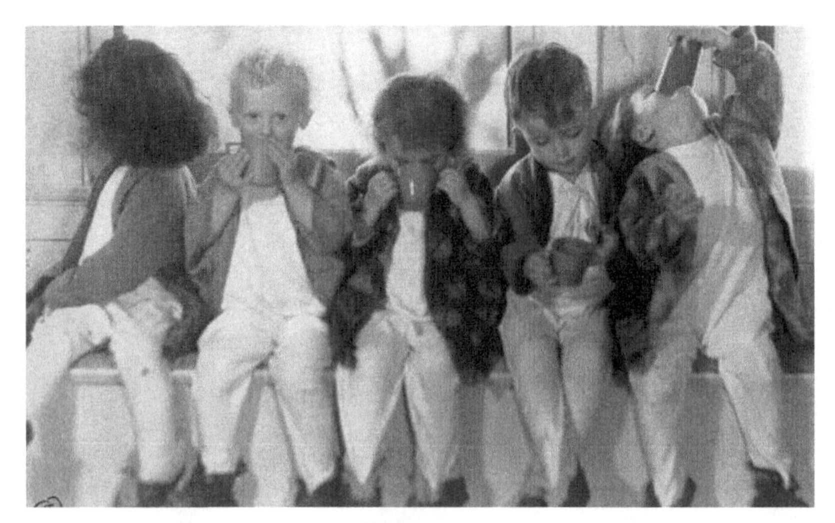

Waking up

Learning to tie shoes

Jan Hill (far left) and Richerd Cancilla (second from far right)

Outdoor art

Outdoor gymnastics

Nursery students painting playhouse outdoors

The Children's Country School
LOS GATOS, CALIFORNIA

CHAPTER 2

THE PARKER RANCH

"...which ever way you come, through Saratoga or Santa Clara, you will be able to find your way to Kennedy Road, off of the San Jose Highway and just inside the Los Gatos city limits, in fact the first road leading to the two white posts down through the orchard...just bring sandwiches and we will serve dessert, tea, and Sanka."

~Mary Orem

Ruth Comfort Mitchell was born in San Francisco and summers were spent in Los Gatos where her parents had summer homes. She launched her literary career by publishing a poem in the Los Gatos Mail newspaper when she was 14 years old. She would go on to be a successful writer of novels, poems, short stories, and plays. She was quite involved with the Los Gatos Christian Church, Los Gatos Pageant, and Los Gatos History Club.[10]

Sanborn Young devoted his energies to politics, photography, and raising racing dogs. A quiet, retiring man who was said to have won his senate seat because of his wife's campaigning, he said of his life, *"My own claim to fame is that I married Ruth Comfort Mitchell"*.[11] The couple made Los Gatos their permanent residence in 1917.

The Senator and his wife had heard of Mary and Elizabeth's nursery school from friends and wanted to meet the women who performed "minor miracles" with so little in the way of supplies or financial support.

Mary writes, *"Senator and Mrs. Sanborn Young (Ruth Comfort Mitchell, the novelist and historian) are giving us a tea around the first of December. Prominent press people, writers, artists, actors, etc are to be asked. It is a divinely lovely thing for them to do, and our only concern is that we have nothing to wear. But something in the way of appropriate clothing is bound to turn up. We would go even if we had to wear our pajamas."*

In 1923, the 38 acre Reilly Ranch in the foothills of Los Gatos was for sale. The ranch was purchased for $6,000 by Colonel James Parker and his wife, Happy. The Colonel was a large man with an even larger personality. He was described by some as a gentler version of Foghorn Leghorn, the larger than life cartoon rooster with a Southern accent. His wife, Happy, was just what her nickname indicated.

Aerial photo of Colonel Parker Ranch

It was at the tea that Mary and Elizabeth learned of the Parker Ranch. It was described as an ideal setting for a real country school with plenty of space for growth. The Senator and his wife knew the Parkers and suggested to Mary that she write the newly retired Colonel on their behalf about purchasing the ranch.

By 1935, the Parker Ranch had shrunk in size from 38 acres to 17 acres. It had a large ten bedroom, five bathroom house referred to by the Colonel as the Barracks. An old rickety tank house, two-bedroom cottage, two story barn, log cabin, stables, and mossed-over tennis court gave promise for growth. A prune and apricot orchard, hawthorns, large spreading Eucalyptus and oak trees nestled in the foothills with a creek winding through made a wide expanse for future gardens and pets of a country school.

Mary wrote to the Colonel inquiring about his ranch. Her letter was ignored. She wrote a second and third letter with no reply from the Colonel. After six months of correspondence and eight more children added to the already over-crowded nursery school, Mary wrote one final letter to the Colonel pleading her case:

PLEASE READ THIS! It is not to beg for anything on earth except a speck of earth you own down here on terms our little fast growing baby school can pay. Won't you see me just a few minutes any day or evening soon and I promise not to pester you. I know the meaning of "no," and I know you are a target for all kinds of hooey. This is REAL and will be the high spot of your years as a philanthropist just to make it possible for our school to BUY this land. Please say when and I'll make it short and snappy.

The Colonel reluctantly agreed to meet Mary. Mary and Elizabeth brought their greatest assets. Seventeen freshly scrubbed and cleanly attired children came to meet the Parkers. The women let the children do their talking. The little ones performed for the Parkers by singing songs, dancing, and playing musical instruments. According to Happy, the Colonel "just melted."

Original 17 students of The Children's Country School

The Parker's daughter had grown up on this ranch. The Colonel had sentimental feelings remembering a place where his once little girl rode horse, climbed trees, and fiddled around in the babbling creek. He thought it a privilege to give over his land to Mary and Elizabeth to be used as a monument for children.

The Parker's sold their ranch for the tidy sum of $20,000. The women needed to raise $2,000 for a down payment. Three parents of the nursery school and the school's newly acquired benefactor, Senator Sanborn Young, combined funds in the amount of $500 each. Mary and Elizabeth also contributed $250 from their newly earned savings.

Leonard Edwards ----------------$500.00
3 year note dated May 25, 1936
6 % interest payable annually
$30.00 should be paid May 25, 1937

Ruth G. Becker------------------$500.00
3 year note dated May 26, 1936
6% interest payable annually
$30.00 should be paid May 26th, 1937

Senator Sanborn Young---------- $500.00
3 year note datedlMay 25, 1936
6% interest payable annually
$30.00 due in May 1937

Nathan Harry Miller------------- $250.00
Two year note dated May 22, 1936
6% interest payable annually
$15.00 due and payable May 22, 1937

Total amount of interest on these notes
to be paid at the end of May 1937 is

$105.00.

Miss Mary Orem paid $250.00 of the $2000.
down payment

Benefactors for Colonel Parker Ranch purchase

Los Gatos

PARKER ESTATE PURCHASED BY COUNTRY SCHOOL

Spacious Residence, 16 Acres Land Now Property Of Local Institution.

Special to the Mercury Herald.

LOS GATOS, June 11.—The 16 acres of rolling land, a spacious residence and other buildings that formed the Colonel James Parker estate on Kennedy road have been sold to the Children's Country school, which has been located on Rose avenue.

The school already has been moved to its new quarters. Teachers will reside in Colonel Parker's guest house.

The school was established here several months ago by Miss Mary Orem who comes from the Lucy Wheelock Kindergarten Training school of Boston and from the Harvard graduate school of education. Miss Elizabeth Glassford, who had several Olympic swimmers in her classes in the east, is athletic instructor. Children from nursery age to 11 years are registered in the school. Features of the training the children receive are music, rhythm, dancing, dramatics, French, arts and crafts and nature study.

The sale was made by the Effie Walton and the McMurtry and Bell real estate offices.

Newspaper clipping of Parker Ranch purchase

There was a grand party with appreciative guests being sung to and who in turn gave toasts of encouragement. The invitation to the celebration was entitled 'Graduation from the Cottage to the Castle.' An article in the Los Gatos Times titled 'Private School on Col. Parker Ranch' quotes Mary, *"It represents everything in location, setting and possibilities for the development of a really different type of children's private school. I am most grateful for the cooperation of parents and friends in making it possible for us to have this property."*[12]

Bill Yabroff, as a 6 year old boy, remembers, *"Walking up to the ranch entrance the grass was so tall, I couldn't see over it. I used to go up on top of the hill and look out on the largest, unbroken, expansive orchard in the world."*

Richerd Cancilla adds, *"I loved growing up here. I loved the whole atmosphere and the trees...just loved the openness. The animals and the horses especially. Just the freedom and to be able to walk around on the hills. This campus is where I grew up and gave me an appreciation and respect for nature. Coming back is like coming home cause it's just a very good comfortable feeling. Feels so good sometimes I like to just stay here and take it all in just pretend that I never left."*

In 1935, Parker Brothers launched their new board game, Monopoly. FDR signed the New Deal. Babe Ruth hit his final home run.[13] And in May, The Children's Country School set permanent roots in Los Gatos.

Cottage to Castle invitation

Bill Yabroff

The Children's Country School

LOS GATOS, CALIFORNIA

CHAPTER 3

DEDICATED

"The support of school friends, the belief in the school, and appreciation of the results as we went along made the early pioneer struggles seem not too hard and wholly worthwhile."

~Mary Orem

Nathalie Wollin with students

Nathalie Wollin brought her two boys Irving, 7, and Bill, 5, to TCCS in 1934. Born in Oakland, CA, she was educated at Mills College. Mills was the first women's college west of the Rockies. An accomplished pianist and singer, Nathalie earned a Bachelor's Degree in Music from Mills with the dream of becoming a professional singer.

Nathalie describes, "*when I first knew it, it was on Rose Avenue on the other side of town and there had been the doctors in San Francisco and Oakland had talked about this grand camp, with recommendations this was the new thing at the time. 'If you want your child to be safe and happy in the country atmosphere, then you have the Children's Country School'. We came to visit and we liked what we saw.*"

After the summer of '34, Nathalie became ill and needed to be hospitalized. She kept her boys at the school for the following school year. When she had recuperated, Nathalie noticed how busy Mary and Elizabeth were on campus taking on multiple roles of housemother, teacher, and administrator. A school day would begin at the crack of dawn and last well past sundown.

The school was in desperate need of a secretary to correspond with parents and visitors to campus. With only one telephone on campus and centrally located within the rarely used tank house, many a phone call was left to ring unanswered. Nathalie was in the midst of a divorce and eager to set roots of her own. She took on the job of secretary, beginning a long tenure at TCCS.

With her extensive background in performing arts, Nathalie soon took over the music and theatre program at the school in which every student played a musical instrument. Robin Clements, a later head of school, describes Nathalie: *"What I remember about Nathalie Wollin is admirable. She was emotionally strong and clear eyed."*

Jan Hill, one of the five original nursery students of the school, states, *"She was a beautiful person…very regal and always pleasant. Miss Wollin had a beautiful singing voice. So unbelievably talented, she could make those Broadway producers move over with the work she did."*

Elizabeth Glassford & Nathalie Wollin with school play performance

Brian Epps, a 1946 graduate of TCCS, offers, "*She really was a marvelous musician and not only that but she helped us to sing. I went on to sing in the men's glee club at UC Berkeley from there to being able to lead a congregation in singing when I was a chaplain. All of this began from Nathalie. It just touches me deeply...to think how that woman poured her life into ours.*"

Mary would be the philosophical leader and day-to day director of school affairs. Epps states, "*Miss Orem was undoubtedly the head of the school. She made that very clear. She was kind to me and helped other children. I never experienced any unkindness from her. But, she was firm and you knew you didn't want to get in trouble with her. Miss Orem gave us a breath of interest in the world.*"

Mariquita West, a 1950 graduate, adds, "*If there is one thing that I carried away from Miss Orem, it would be a very deep sense of ethics and idealism. I think values of honesty, responsibility, sportsmanship, kindness really stuck.*"

Bill Yabroff describes Mary as "*a very strong woman. Very stern. As a boy, she was someone I was afraid of, and on the other sense, I loved her dearly. She was an incredible teacher...very practical. There was just so many good things that she did I'll never forget. She gave me a rocket start in my life. She would say to me 'Do you want to be someone or just anyone?'*"

Mary Orem with boarding children

Mary Orem teaching

Elizabeth would take on many hats at the school from swim instructor to bus driver and from cook to gardener. Jan Hill says of Elizabeth, *"We could call her the humanitarian of the group. She was a lovely person. And she taught us to swim and never saw her in the water except one time at the beach and she actually dove in and saved a man's life."*

Epps says of Elizabeth, *"I see her in my mind walking around the campus always in slacks keeping the whole business running. She was like the general in charge of the camp there and she oversaw all of the activities from cooking to laundry to cleaning whatever it was to run the place it was Miss Glassford who took charge. She also was the one who fixed us if we had a cut or scrape. She was always good-natured, always had a kind word."*

Elizabeth is described by the children as always cheery, and, in fact, Cheery became her nickname among adults. Yabroff adds, *"She had a sense of humor. She wasn't a disciplinarian. All the kids loved her. She was a beautiful person."*

Richerd Cancilla describes a birthday tradition at the school started by Elizabeth. *"It was kind of a tradition to give you a spanking on your birthday with a baseball bat all in fun, of course. I would write to my father and say Miss Glassford is giving me a spanking today because it's my birthday."*

Elizabeth Glassford driving school "bus"

Elizabeth Glassford nicknamed "Cheery"

In 1934, Masako Ishida was earning her teaching credential from the State Teacher's College of San Jose. She would be the first Japanese-American to receive a teaching credential from the State Teacher's College, now known as San Jose State University. At 20 years old, she joined TCCS in the summer of 1935 and became the housemother to the 23 resident children.

Jan Hill remembers, "*She was there and she was always kind and always caring. You knew she was a good person inside.*" Clements remembers Saki visiting the school in later years. "*She came down from Sacramento and loved to reminisce. And what she remembered was the life in the dormitory. She remembered the boys and girls who lived in the dorms. She was very fond of them because she was their mother. In a very important way, she raised these boys and girls.*"

Miss Saki

The word used repeatedly to describe Saki by the three women was simply: dedicated. So dedicated, that she was respectfully named a silent partner, and fondly, the fifth founder of TCCS.

The fourth founder of TCCS joined the school in 1942. Ann Boge was born in San Francisco in 1889. The daughter of Danish immigrants, she was raised with a love of the traditions of the old country. She worked for many years as an executive secretary for a major steamship line. When the Depression hit, she and her sister Alma took their savings and bought a small chicken ranch in Palo Alto, CA.

Ann met Mary and Elizabeth at a Christian Scientist meeting. She was impressed with their ideas on education and the three women became fast friends. She soon joined TCCS as a classroom teacher. She would be given the nickname of Aunt Ann. Clements met Ann Boge in her later years. *"She was a real study. She sat bolt upright. She was about a thousand years old. And she had eyes like an eagle with clear blue eyes, very Danish-looking. She would sort of stare at you, but didn't say very much."*

Bill Yabroff, son of Nathalie Wollin, says of Ann, *"She taught morals...right and wrong. She had great patience. She took the students who were behind and tutored them."* The special needs students under her guidance would affectionately be known as 'Aunt Ann's Boys.'

Ann Boge

Ann held geography classes in her upstairs room in the Sara Heavenrich Cottage around big picnic tables where adolescent students played footsie under the table. Two students, Bill and Audrey, whose last names will remain anonymous, were found kissing and sentenced to two days in isolation for punishment. The children remember Elizabeth and Ann listening to Stella Dallas radio shows everyday during nap time. Movies like Swiss Family Robinson, would be shown in her room some nights. The children remember it being such a treat to sit on the floor with the lights turned out eating popcorn with friends. One student recalled that Aunt Ann read a story like you never heard before...Wind in the Willows she can still hear today.

Mary Orem, Elizabeth Glassford, Nathalie Wollin, and Ann Boge would be known as the four founders of TCCS. All four women would not take a salary for ten years. TCCS was not only their workplace, but their home. They dedicated their lives to the school and the partnership that bound them together.

Ann Boge & Elizabeth Glassford

Elizabeth Glassford & Miss Saki with children on a field trip

Betty's painting a purple Cow. Janet's modeling dishes now. Stuart's building a barn.

CHAPTER 4

PARKER RANCH GETS A FACELIFT

"Facing the tremendous undertaking of getting ready a plant to accommodate children put steel into muscles and starch into endurance."

~Mary Orem

It was a time of growth and settlement for TCCS. True to Mary's forward thinking, the campus was about to get a needed facelift. Though large in acreage, the ranch primarily existed west of the creek. The smell of oil and sound of gravel on rushing feet was experienced throughout the campus as walkways and roads became apparent. The large, rickety water tower received much needed attention. The tank was removed from the top level and a bedroom was added to the space. The bottom of the tower became Mary's office. An additional room with fireplace was added to the base of the tower, which became a music room for music lessons and rehearsals.

The water tower with attached music room and kitchen & dining hall in the background

Perpendicular to the tower was the setting for a would-be swimming pool. The pool would be fed by the creek that ran south near the tower. The pool became a necessary commodity with Elizabeth being a competitive swimmer and soon to be swim instructor. The creek had been dammed and was released in order to be fed into the newly constructed swimming pool. The creek also provided water for outdoor showers that were added at the same time as the pool. A concrete bridge was constructed to allow access over the creek to the east side of campus. A stable and barn were resurrected across the bridge. Even Hans and Gretel were put to work hunting rattlesnakes and tarantulas among the rolling hills.

Elizabeth Glassford at the swimming pool

An outdoor brick patio was added in front of the kitchen. The patio included an outdoor fireplace with T.C.C.S chiseled on the bricks above the opening. The patio was adjacent to the dining hall which included a small stage for practicing school plays. The school purchased 12' X 18' voting tents to use as outdoor sleeping quarters for older children. The tents consisted of wood floors and canvas awnings that could house five bunk beds. Many a story was shared by students about scary, but ultimately entertaining, evenings filled with flashes and booms of thunder and lightning.

Soon a generous donation by Sara Heavenrich, the grandmother of a boarding student, provided for a two story building to be built across the creek. Legend tells of Heavenrich's grandson being quite the handful and

Boys standing in front of sleeping tents

the building being a peace offering by her to allow him to remain a resident student at the school. Known as Sara Heavenrich Cottage, the U-shaped building contained a fireplace, living room, and upstairs bedroom.

The Tower and Sara Heavenrich Cottage would be remembered by the students for another reason. Disciplinary action was usually in one of two forms: sit on the steps or walk the beat. The steps were those that lead to the top of the Tower. You were to sit on the steps for all to see as they went about their business on campus. "Walking the beat was making a track around Sara Heavenrich Cottage usually with a piece of poetry in your hands to memorize and later recite with precision.

Sara Heavenrich Cottage

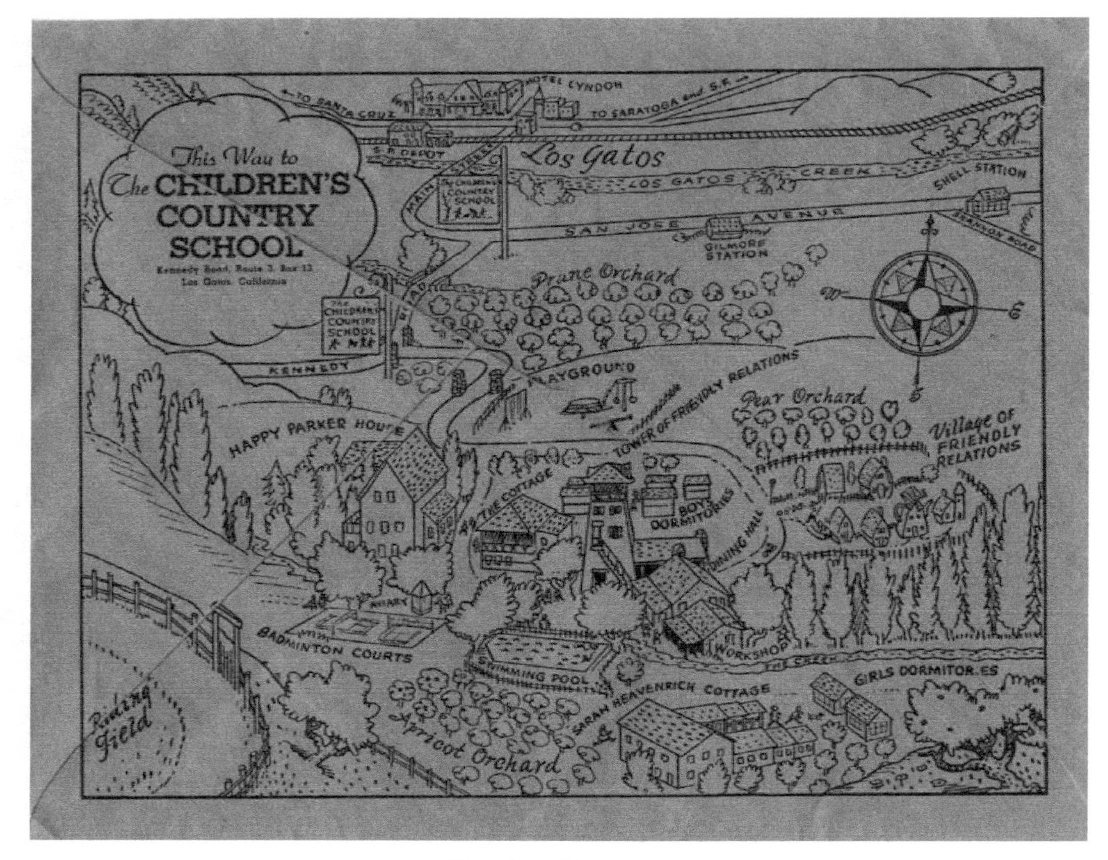

Drawing of Campus

A Message From Pied Piper's Call

Los Gatos, California

CHAPTER 5

THE PIED PIPER'S CALL

"Summer in the sunshine of the blossom-laden foothills of Los Gatos far away from the city strife under the stars around evening campfire glow of sweet friendships shared... doing all of the things you have dreamed of for years."

~The Pied Piper's Call brochure

With the necessary roads and building renovations completed on campus, the school was ready to host a summer camp that would continually bring the school financial solvency, as well as enjoy a world renowned notoriety. The nine week camp would hold double the size of its school enrollment ranging from 75 kids in 1936 to as many as 125 in the 1940's.

The Pied Piper's Call invited campers to *"come with your suitcase and toothbrush and talents of all shapes and sizes…to share in the adventures of horseback riding, a sunny pool, campfire songs, stunts, folk dancing, nature hikes up woody trails, building, modeling, painting, weaving in the craft shop, sun baths, and good food."*

The camp's main attraction was horseback riding. The riding instructor, Bob Thompson, was beloved by the children. He was described as a rough and tumble cowboy with a heart of gold. Children tell the story of Thompson having kids hold on to the electric fence that divided part of the property. The children would hold hands while standing in a circle. The last person to join the circle would get the shock. The kids always ran to be the first on the fence for good reason. This also became a way of initiating new arrivals to the camp by resident children. Each summer older students proudly rode the three miles into Los Gatos with Thompson to join the Fourth of July parade, as well as to demonstrate intricate riding formations at the school rodeos.

The names of the horses are still recited in an instant by these grown children. Horses and ponies with such names as Misty, Lady Luck, Peaches, Sally White, Inky, and Helen of Troy. An offspring to the great racing horse, Citation, was the fastest. Patches was the most temperamental. Black Beauty and Sundance were so old it took all their energy just to swat away flies with their tails. Kids played cowboys and Indians on the Shetland ponies. A student who learned to mount a horse from the left side continued this practice with a bicycle and later motorcycle. One horseback rider

—friendships
—to help your group make this year's Pied Piper's Call the best yet
—exciting out-of-doors times doing all of the things you have dreamed of doing .
counselors and leaders
—to know that you're well and safe so they won't worry about you
—to know that you're happy and getting along with your Group
—to know that you're learning a lot of new Things

—then listen, — The Pied Piper's Call

"Get up, sleepy-head. Get ready for that big Country Breakfast."
Camp Chores are fun when everyone helps to tidy-up.

Now for the day's program.
Off on Horseback along winding trails—after you learn to manage your horse.

Camp Crafts—a time to put that "good idea" into form—with clay, weaving, paints or wood.

Photography—where you learn to take "good" pictures—develop and print them—and enlarge your favorite ones.

Group free time to read a story
play games
or just lie out in the sun and talk.

Sports—building toward the All-camp Jr. Olympics
Archery . . . Tennis . . . Basket and Volleyball
Baseball . . . Boxing . . . Track.

the after lunch quiet hour in the Group tent gives time to listen to good music, good reading—or learn to listen for the small Nature sounds of the Countryside.

Swimming time—a lesson, practice for Red Cross swimming tests and Junior Olympics—and "free swim" time.

Hikes through fields and wooded countryside bringing back Things for your Nature collection.

Fishing Trips to Anderson Dam with some of your pals—after you learn to manage the boat.

and in between those mid-morning and afternoon snacks are welcome—even though you did have seconds for lunch.

All-Camp Projects may be
—felling logs and building a pioneer cabin or engineering a bridge over the creek,
—erecting and painting a big Indian Tepee for camp council or building a Pond for the Ducks and the Geese.
—"doing all of the things you have dreamed of for years."

The evening times—after dinner—
Campfire, singing, stunts, and folk dancing.
Camp council . . . evening vespers—

"Far away from the city strife—under the stars,
Around evening camp fire glow,
Good friendship shared, things real as they are."

remembers the view from the eastward hill seeing White Tower hamburger in downtown Los Gatos. Another student recalls the memorable ride into the small agricultural town of Los Gatos among what seemed like endless groves of orange trees.

Bill Yabroff was a camper in those early years who explained the freedom of horseback riding without supervision. I asked how the founders could trust the kids to horseback ride alone. My question stopped Bill in his tracks. He told me in a stern, but matter of fact manner, that if you said you were going to do something, then you did it...and if you didn't do what you said, then you lost that privilege for good. A simple lesson of ample importance.

The camp became well-known far beyond its rolling hills home. Children spent their summer at TCCS from all over the United States. And during the war years, the campers came from all over the world. Yabroff remembers the son of the Ambassador of Australia after seeing shredded wheat for the first time exclaiming, *"This is biscuits with hair on them!"*

The camp would take a week long trip to South Lake Tahoe. The Presbyterian Conference Grounds at Zephyr Cove is located a few miles from Stateline within a stones throw of the lake. An early telegram sent by Elizabeth from Lake Tahoe back to Mary reads: *"ARRIVED AFTER SIX STOP HAD TWO HOURS REST STOP CHILDREN ALL ARRIVED AFTER SIX STOP SAFELY IN BED STOP"*

Zephyr Point in Lake Tahoe Brochure[14]

Preparing to horseback ride

A horseback rider

The Shetland ponies

Students learning to ride

Riding the Shetland ponies

Horseback riding with instructor Bob Thompson

Lake Tahoe was where the children learned how to canoe and eat fresh trout from their daily fishing excursions. One summer saw a dozen children climb to the top of Mount Tallac, with an elevation 9,739 ft. The large lake became a giant pool for swim lessons. And the stairs to the dormitory became the temporary "sit on the steps" punishment for over-exuberant children.

Children atop Mount Tallac

Elizabeth writes, "*Here we are in the most beautiful place in the world with the lake several shades of blue and the pine trees growing right down to the shore line almost…while 57 children cavort among pines and eat tremendous amounts of perfectly grand food. The nursery is on the beach playing and swimming all morning, then have dinner, and sleep three hours. After supper, they stay awake for the assembly with the other children and it is a real thrill for them as we have stunts, singing, musical chairs, charades, etc.*"

As exciting as Lake Tahoe was for the children, the school purchased their own oasis closer to Los Gatos. A beach house 30 miles away in Santa Cruz, CA became a new attraction for campers to learn and explore with sand castles, crabs, shell collecting, and sunbathing for healthy vitamin D sunlight.

The trip to the beach house became an adventure all to itself. The school owned a station wagon that obviously could not accommodate all of the campers. Later, the school would purchase a pickup truck to help transport children to Santa Cruz. Mariquita West recalls, *"I remember driving down there in the back of a truck with the kids lined up on benches. Can you imagine trying to do that now?"*

The trip would start with the youngest children being loaded into the station wagon and driven to Santa Cruz. The rest of the camp would begin walking towards Santa Cruz taking Old San Jose Road as their foot path. Elizabeth, the pseudo bus driver, would drop off the youngest children at the Beach House, as well as Miss Saki, and then head back to Los Gatos to pick up the next oldest children who were walking.

In the eyes of then 14 year old Richerd Cancilla and Jan Hill, this was an opportunity to not only be leaders of the excursion, but eventually be left alone, or more pointedly, absent of adult supervision. The walk was not a laboring experience, but rather an exciting adventure of their own creation. They both recall walking with Summit Road in view before being picked up by Elizabeth's station wagon. Summit Road was some 12 miles away.

The summer camp was the main source of income for keeping the school solvent through out its academic school years. Year after year, the Pied Piper's Call turned a deficit into a surplus. Nathalie would later say that some schools had endowments, we had a summer camp.

Elizabeth Glassford handing out a coke in Lake Tahoe

Children in TCCS summer uniforms

Children travelling to Santa Cruz

Summer camp group photo at Santa Cruz Beach House

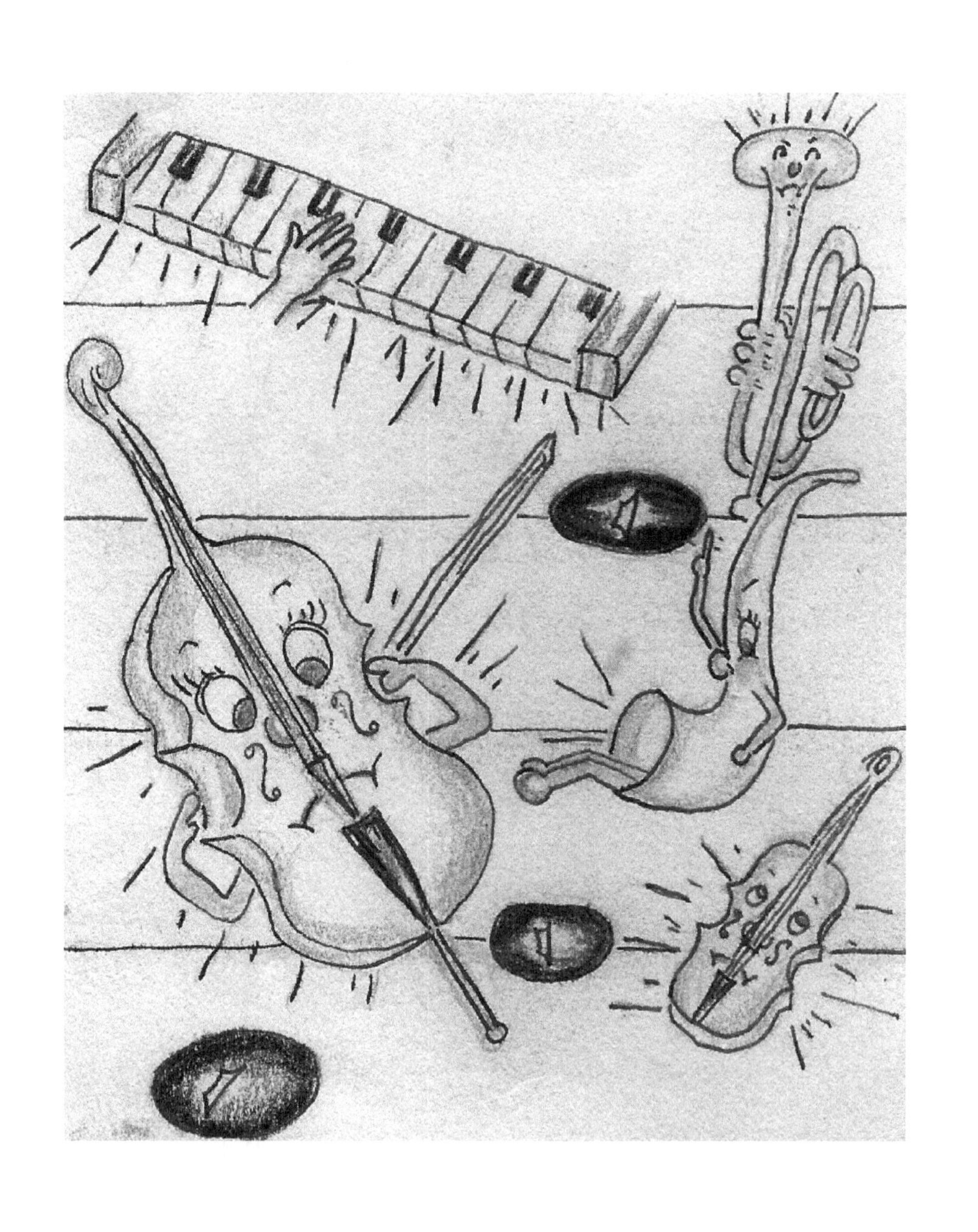

CHAPTER 6

LEARNING BY DOING

"It has always been her dream to bring every child out to the place where he may express himself through his medium. I don't know of any other place around here that is giving the very rich program to all of its children as is Miss Orem."

~Nathalie Wollin

After a successful summer camp, TCCS was ready to start its first academic school year. Mary writes *"Our tuition is $800 for the school year for the boarding child which will include room and board, laundry, supervision of studies, riding and swimming during the nice weather. Horses and swimming are in the school curriculum. The children are grouped according to social age and the school curriculum follows pretty much the requirements of the State. As I believe I explained to you, the children do not have individual rooms. They sleep in the tents in double deckers in groups and the dressing rooms are for the groups. We do maintain careful supervision and guidance and hold to a high achievement pattern both in school and in the family living group.*

There is usually one home-weekend a month, which starts on Thursdays and the children return on Monday morning. This makes it possible for the children who live some distance to have some time at home. The child would of course be home for the Thanksgiving, Christmas, and Easter vacations."

As the student body grew, so did the faculty out of necessity. The boarding school teacher would be a unique breed who was not only outdoors savvy, but able to juggle responsibilities as both a teacher and surrogate mother. Recruiting letters were sent out focusing on the "women's Ivy League" or the "Seven Sisters" schools: Vassar, Wellesley, Smith, Bryn Mawr, Barnard, Radcliffe, and Mt. Holyoke. By 1937, the school had added five young teachers who headed west from their east coast residences.

One recruitment letter reads, *"The school is not endowed, so our salaries can't compete with the public schools, but there is great opportunity for creative work with the children and to help train children on the superior side for the leadership which our country will need as we go on…Because of the country life we live, the need to be physically strong must be considered. Also, the teacher must have real enthusiasm for children… progressive ideas of teaching, a pleasing personality* *and Protestant preferred. Age does not matter if she has the above qualifications...The salary a total of $100 is divided into an estimated $45 room, board, and laundry...and a $55 cash renumeration with opportunity as the school grows for working into the organization as a real part of a cooperative basis."*

1936 Faculty

The school day began with children awakening at 6 am. Bryan Epps explains "*Our sleeping quarters were expanded tents with wooden floors and half screened sides with canvas flaps so we could lower them in rainy weather. Each tent had several double decker beds.*

Our day began with jumping up making the bed quickly, pulling on our jeans; getting the horses from the corral; putting a halter on one and riding it bareback to the stables. We learned about horses; how to brush and curry them; saddle and bridle them; clean their hooves in the stable; how to ride them. We prepared the horses and rode them later in the day." Besides the care for horses, children also moved freely about in the morning feeding and caring for chickens, ducks, goats, pigs, and rabbits.

The nursery and primary school children slept in the ten bedroom Barracks, or newly named, Big House. The nursery children slept in spacious bedrooms indoors, while the primary students slept on bunk beds on the front porch of the house with screens extending from the roof gutters to the porch railings to keep bugs out. These children also had chores, like carrying milk bottles, cleaning the dressing rooms, and helping in the kitchen and dining hall to set up for breakfast.

Epps continues, "*After these chores, we headed for the showers. They were outdoors in a brick enclosure by the pool. We had to soap up from head to foot and scrub with small stiff brushes before we were allowed to rinse off.*"

The showers became a lasting memory for all. Nathalie writes, "*We could take them down to the pool every morning for a cold shower. Some of them still remember it with horror, I guess. Oh, they were healthy. Little rocks!*"

Epps continues, "*We then ran back to our dressing rooms and put on our usual uniform. There were green (corduroy) sets and brown sets, as I recall. We changed once a week, but we always felt splendid in our new set.*

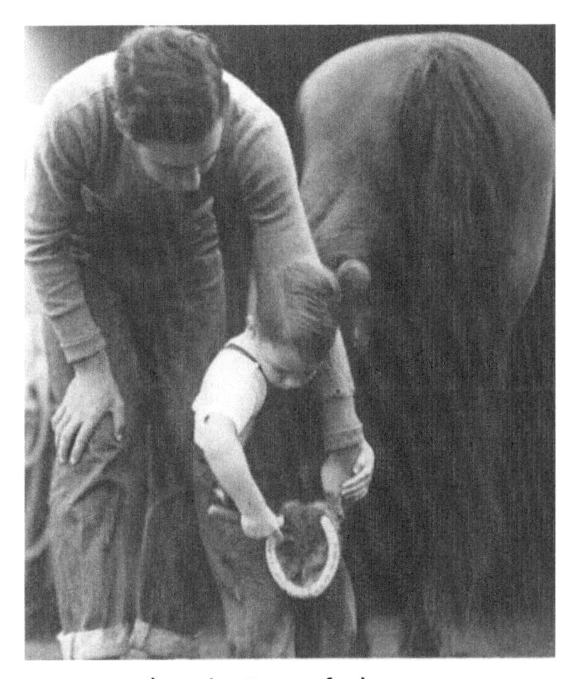

Learning to care for horses

Farm animals on campus

Daily morning showers outdoors

Children in dark green corduroy uniforms

Next, came breakfast in the dining hall. All the children in the school ate there at the same time. It was a large room with a stage on one side for our theater productions. We took turns being dining room managers, whose job it was to set out all the dishes and silverware on the long tables and then bring the food from the kitchen. Most mornings we had oatmeal, but on weekends we often had pancakes or french toast and sometimes scrambled eggs.

Being dining room manager was fun and we got to go into the kitchen and the cook gave us extra treats. Our cook was Mr. Robertson, a Scotsman, who stood about 6'1". The kitchen ceiling was about 5'10", so he was always bent over slightly. He often quoted Robert Browning in his thick Scottish brogue, 'A man's a man for all that and all that.'"

All meals were held in the dining hall. Meals were a time when a family-structure was instilled by Mary. At each set of round tables sat an adult with a group of children. A purposely placed piano in the room provided live music ambiance. Table manners and conversation etiquette were strictly enforced. Students were instructed to stand at their chair until teachers and adults sat down first. You then sat straight up with hands in your lap.

Left over dry toast from breakfast would be left outside the kitchen to be snacked on by students as they moved throughout campus in the morning. One student still prepares stewed prunes and dried apricots for breakfast, as well as leaving dried toast out for her own children to snack on. One student remembers the lesson to always eat your meat last so that you eat all of your vegetables. This practice was passed on to her own children, as well.

The dining hall

TCCS had many students that had connections to the food industry both directly and indirectly. Jan Hill was known to many households as the cute baby on the outside of the Cream of Wheat box. Sharon Kellogg, Peter Heinz, and Marjorie Post were all children whose last names directly linked them to the cereal and condiment companies. During WWII, a Post cereal delivery truck over-turned outside of Modesto, CA. The dented and damaged boxes of cereal were donated to TCCS. For months, children enjoyed, and or tolerated, bowls of Grape Nuts and Post's newest product, Raisin Bran.[15] The Skippy Peanut Butter Company in Alameda, CA began in 1933.[16] Its founder sent his son to TCCS. His name was Skippy.

Jan Hill, the Cream of Wheat baby[17]

After breakfast, academic classes would take up the morning followed by a sit down lunch in the dining hall. Before classes in the afternoon, the children would have a rest period which consisted of either, playing, napping, sunbathing, or practicing a musical instrument. Afternoon classes would conclude at 4 pm.

Henry Van Loon's A Story of Mankind was the text book used for social science. He was not known as a typical textbook writer of the times. As a writer, he emphasized crucial historical events and gave a complete picture of individual characters, as well as the role of the arts in history. He also had an informal and thought-provoking style which, particularly in The Story of Mankind, included personal anecdotes.[18]

Children performed chores before dinner such as caring for animals, working in their gardens, and tidying up the campus. After dinner, time was spent doing homework, practicing instruments, and reading. All children were in bed by 8 pm. On weekends, bedtime was extended to allow for sing-alongs in the dining hall or an occasional movie with popcorn.

Mary Orem with children doing chores

Children gardening

Children chopping wood

A devastating measles epidemic hit the Bay Area in 1937 that stretched from San Francisco north to Los Gatos south. Many students remember the measles epidemic as a time when they learned to play the harmonica. The epidemic, along with the still gripping effects of the Depression, soon closed nearby private schools such as Top of the Hill School.[19] Top of the Hill School sat on top of Kennedy Road above TCCS over looking Santa Clara Valley. Since TCCS was a boarding school, it was able to quarantine its students. Cast offs from recently closed Top of the Hill School were added to its growing student body. This episode would begin TCCS' standing as the oldest co-ed private elementary school in Santa Clara County.

The school emphasized a program of learning by doing. Whether this method of learning applied to measuring a trough for vegetable irrigation or playing a violin, knowledge was not restricted to the classroom. Mary writes, "*Have you ever seen the beauty that comes into a student's eyes when he has reasoned through a problem to the satisfactory answer? It transcends the physical glorifying the plainest face.*"

Nathalie's role as secretary had naturally evolved into school musical director. Under Nathalie's direction, every student in the school played a musical instrument while also learning to read music. From cello to piano to violin, children were immersed in Nathalie's love of music. Music also became a daily part of life. Children sang at meals, to and from class, and at night before bed to encourage the feel of family.

Measles-free children playing harmonica

Nathalie Wollin leading a sing-along

Mary writes, "*We are working up a small children's symphony right here in the school. I believe I told you that we have an exceptionally fine teacher and the boys will have a very fine musical background. Of course, the Music Theory Department is humming overtime, creating music, and introducing every child in the school, from 18 months on, to the language of Music. We are truly becoming a center for creative Art and Music.*"

In 1938, a curly-haired three year old was waking up from his nap in the Big House. Miss Saki recounted what happened next: "*Sammy walked right over to the piano and he just started playing.*" Samuel Lipman, a child prodigy, verified this same story in an interview that he gave in 1978. Lipman would give his first public recital at the age of 8 at the Curran Theater in San Francisco. Lipman writes, "*I don't think I had heard a live symphony orchestra before I played a concerto with one at the age of eleven.*"[20] Samuel Lipman went on to become an accomplished pianist and music critic.

Music lessons

Outdoor music recital

Child prodigy Sammy Lipman

The school plays would be a product of Nathalie's music program and its marriage with theatre. These elaborate spring performances, as well as annual performances during the Pied Piper's Call, involved the entire student body and basically suspended academic classes in place of preparation for the play. From Alice in Wonderland to the The Blue Bird to Pirates of Penzance, students still recall these plays with youthful enthusiasm as the highlight of the school year. Mariquita West adds, *"I loved the plays. I just adored that...I loved the Spring...being outdoors...the whole way they did it."*

The school plays were originally directed by Dorothea Johnston. Johnston was a former Shakespearian actor who in her extensive career had performed for the Queen of England. Johnston owned the outdoor Theater in the Glade which was part of the Saratoga Inn. Johnston was known as the drama teacher to Olivia de Havilland. It was the role of Puck, under Johnston's direction of Midsummer's Night Dream, in which de Havilland was discovered by a Hollywood agent.

Some students recall de Havilland helping out Johnston with TCCS's performance of Midsummer's Night Dream in Saratoga. One student in particular remembers Olivia taking an interest in his peanut butter sandwich just before going on stage and her winking at him as he did his best acting as a tree on stage. With Johnston as the director of the school plays, these performances were quite elaborate and well-attended in the town of Saratoga.

TCCS would have three families with ties to the entertainment industry. Yehudi Menuhin, world-renown violinist and resident of Los Gatos, sent his two sons annually to the Pied Piper's Call summer camp. June Havoc, actress and sister of Gypsie Rose Lee, sent her actress-to-be daughter April to the school. Havoc, active on the road with her dance act when not making movies, wrote frequently to her daughter. One letter reads *"April, darling...here I am in New Orleans, of all places. I'm doing about five weeks of personal appearances...remember when you used to sit in the wings and watch my act? Well, it's the same thing."*[21]

Hedy Lamarr's children, Tony and Denise, attended the school in the early 1940's. Lamarr stayed at the Hotel Lyndon in Los Gatos when visiting her children. Tom Watkins says Lamarr, *"with her mink coat, was down-to-earth friendly,"* taking him and her two children to Foster Freeze across from Los Gatos High School to get 25 cent double decker ice cream cones.

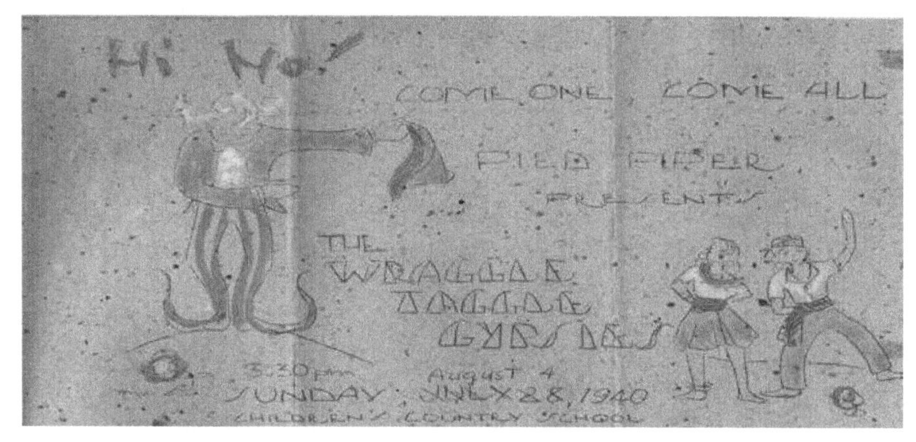

***The Gypsies* play performance program**

***Alice in Wonderland* play performance program**

After Johnston retired, the plays were directed and scored by Nathalie. Some of these plays were original productions, like The Gypsies, with all the music and lyrics written by Nathalie. The tryouts for the plays were a little unconventional. Students did not try out for one part, but rather every part.

Bryan Epps, who played Lysander in Midsummer's Night Dream, recalls the tryout process. "*Preparation for every play began with each of us learning all the lines. The play was typed out and the pages were cut into small numbered strips which we then took and memorized as we walked around the grounds and through the orchards. When we memorized one strip, we had to recite all of the play up to and including that last strip. We raced to see who could finish first. At one time, I could recite all of A Midsummer's Night Dream. We tried out for the roles by reciting passages before the rest of the school. School director, Mary Orem, held her hand over each would-be actor and the one who received the most applause got the part. I always felt that Miss Orem somehow encouraged applause for those best suited for the role.*"

The production was now in motion. Costumes were made, sets were designed, and performers took their roles seriously knowing that two or three understudies were ready to take their part if they were not able to meet Nathalie's high standards. Field trips were taken to San Francisco to provide the students with an opportunity to see a live stage performance. The students would cram into the school station wagon and head down the highway to San Francisco.

Nathalie writes "*We went to the opera in San Francisco on Monday night with 26 of us all dressed up and thrilled; flowers in our hair and everything. Jane was perfectly beautiful with her golden hair tucked back with pink flowers and a light blue dress, new white slippers and radiant face. We heard Lily Pons in Rigoletto and the performance was superb in every detail. It will be something the children will always remember, I'm sure.*"

The plays were practiced on campus on a small stage in the cafeteria before they were performed for a live audience in Saratoga. Each student in the school played a role. Whether they were a still body behind a picture frame hanging on the wall in The Little Minister or a nursery student playing a flower in The Blue Bird, each student was a member of the cast.

A black and white 8 mm film exists of a 1938 production of the Wind in the Willows. This film shows the pageantry and use of dance and music in an outdoor setting. Students portraying trees blowing in the wind sway in the background. Nursery children act as flowers while ballerinas dance around in the forest scenery.

Clare Yabroff, grand daughter of Nathalie and student at TCCS, describes the theatre program. *"I really had no idea at the time what the value was. The performing arts are immediate. You have immediate consequences for your actions. If you lose focus; if you don't learn your lines; if you don't work together; you have immediate result. What the children learned in terms of confidence and being in front of people...of learning great literature... the value, I think, is immeasurable. She came from a background of theatre and performing. She knew the value of it for young children."*

Nursery students on stage for *The Gypsies* performance

Children practicing for play performance

Cast of *The Gypsies*

Wind in the Willows performance outdoors

Paul Robeson[22]

Learning by doing included guests descending on the school to expose the children to experiences foreign to their daily routines. E.E. Kellogg of Alaska brought his Alaskan sled dogs to campus. Imagine being an 8 year old and being led through campus on a sled by a pack of six Husky dogs. Yehudi Menuhin was a frequent visitor as a father and performer on campus. He would bring his accompanist, Adolph Baller, to perform with him for the children. Paul Robeson, singer and activist, gave a singing performance in the indoor dining hall. Bill Yabroff, a nine year old at the time, recalls a famous bird caller teaching voice pitch by placing a wine glass at one end of the room and hitting a note that caused the glass to shatter. All of these events continue to reverberate in the memory of these grown children.

Olivia de Havilland & Yehudi Menuhin[23]

Yabroff adds "*when they came we would all sit around them and we could ask them any questions like how they learned to sing. It was very informal. It wasn't like a 20 minute thing. It would last for hours....I don't know how she (Mary) got them.*"

Annual field trips included those to Lake Tahoe and Yosemite for winter break. Elizabeth writes about "*sitting up on what seems to be the top of*

E.E. Kellogg and his Alaskan sled

the world watching the ski lift coming down. It is very beautiful with the very tall pine trees and long shadows coming through the trees and sunshine on all sides of us. There goes Janet falling all over herself, up she picks herself and away again. Oh, there goes Walter calling his ski is broken, he is coming back like a lame duck."

Mary wanted to be sure that the children's growing comes from their own doing. This was evident in their learning to ski, fish, canoe, ride horses, and start a camp fire. The children were exposed to the arts as it surrounded them in its natural essence. From an elaborate Opera House to a simple wooden dining hall, Mary wanted *"a rich background of the cultural things which will enable them to contribute or to draw about them as friends those who are contributors in music, art, literature and economics."*

The report card of the school would reflect the vision of learning by doing. The title atop the report card reads Right Habits are Outgrowth of Right Attitudes. The children were evaluated on academic abilities, as well as personal and social habits. These habits were observed on a 24/7 basis with teachers taking on the dual role of teacher and parent.

Yosemite ski trip

Elizabeth Glassford with children on a field trip

The first area of reflection on the report card was Social Habits. These habits could include one word character traits such as leadership, cooperation, adaptability, courage, and obedience. Social habits could also be more descriptive like "helps to make school a happier place," "asks permission to use the belongings of others and returns them in good condition,"; and "obedience to own ideals and to others commands."

The second area of reflection was Personal Habits. This topic covered manners, personal responsibility, and character. The earliest report card of TCCS evaluates manners by asking if the student says: "good morning, good afternoon, good evening, pardon me, please, thank you, May I help you?, and I am sorry." Personal responsibility is measured by "shoe tying, clean fingernails, closing doors quietly, standing and walking properly, folds and hangs up clothes properly, makes a smooth bed, and learning to eat many different foods." The student's character is evaluated by traits of "loyalty, generosity, tolerance, reliability, poise, stability, vigor, and happy disposition."

The third area of reflection was Scholastic Progress. This was the academic portion of the report card. Subjects include reading, language experiences, number experiences, natural sciences, social sciences, French experiences, appreciative experiences (music, dramatics, art, poetry), and extra experiences (private music, riding, swimming). One area of study that was added during the WWII years was Defense Program, evaluating farm work and home economics.

The areas of academic study are not just given a letter grade, but rather a descriptive sentence to measure progress. For reading, a child was evaluated on whether he/she makes reading interesting to those who listen. In social sciences, students were gauged to show an active interest in the Weekly News Reader and if curious about the earth, its origin, and its people. Natural Sciences mirrors today's sense of appreciation and conservation of nature by asking if the student observes and enjoys nature, as well as protects and conserves nature.

Nathalie writes, "*We believe that the establishment of the qualities of honesty, reliability, the habits of care and concentration are all forerunners to the making of a good student and a desirable companion.*" Mary concludes, "*Be sure that the children's growing comes from their own doing of learning by doing...to build up enough resources within themselves to live ensemble or alone and be happy with feeling of universality...for the ultimate goal of education is to benefit society...for graduation from TCCS means attaining certain standards in character growth, as scholastic growth.*"

The first graduation from TCCS in 1939 consisted of three graduates. During the ceremony, each student read their "prophesy" or glimpse into their future. Bud Williamson wrote of owning a dude ranch in Nevada. Vervaleen Trogden prophesized owning a big house with servants. Marilyn Mitchell would be a successful secretary in Paris. Each story had a similar theme of a lamp of truth and love keeping them grounded and unselfish.

The theme of a lamp of truth and love would become an integral part of graduation in the near future. A gold graduation ring would be given to graduates. The ring had TCCS inscribed on the side and a crest consisting of the lamp of truth and love sitting on top of the book of knowledge which encompassed the world globe with olive branches cradling the world for healing of nations and peace.

Mary's closing remarks of the graduation ceremony; "*From this mother lamp, symbolic of our watchwords truth and love, we are lighting your little candles to carry with you into your futures. Carry these lights high and joyously. Without Truth there is only wilderness—without Love, life has no purpose.*"

In 1939, Nathalie wrote the school song which became the anthem for future graduations:

At the Children's Country School, I'll always remember
The happy children's voices raised in song
Where the lamp of truth and love is gently kindled
To light our paths in all the days to come

Our cradle school in the foothills of Los Gatos
Those sunny happy days of work and play
Making pals of friendliness and cooperation
Finding hidden treasures in each busy day

Dear Children's Country School, we sing your praises
For as the twig is bent, the tree will grow
Your fine ideals will be forever with us
And through our actions, your dear light will grow

HAPPY TIMES

CHILDREN'S COUNTRY SCHOOL LOS GATOS

Special Edition by SENIOR class June 4 '39

GRADUATED!

From this Mother Lamp, symbolic of our watchwords TRUTH and LOVE, we are lighting your little candles to carry with you into your futures. Carry these lights high and joyously. Without TRUTH there is only a wilderness----without LOVE, life has no purpose.

" AND MAY THE LOVE OF GOD WHICH PASSETH ALL UNDERSTANDING BE WITH YOU NOW AND FOREVERMORE."

With this message from Miss Orem ringing in our ears, we found ourselves graduated!

1939 Graduation edition of Happy Times

Graduation ring insignia design

Mary Orem's closing remarks at 1946 Graduation ceremony

Pied Piper's Boot Camp

a little children's world
where you really belong—
where you make pals of
friendliness and cooperation

— —

CHAPTER 7

THE VILLAGE OF FRIENDLY RELATIONS

"Now, he is one of that world. A world of children, who have their own community, are respected as individuals, are encouraged to do their own thinking; see their child dreams come true in their own creating, and with it all know what is going on about them in the adult world so as to gain a true sense of values and their relationship to that world into which some day they must become a part."

~Mary Orem

In 1937, Mary had a vision to create a miniature town that would be a training ground for the children to learn life skills for becoming the leaders of tomorrow. Mary would incorporate her vast learning and practical experiences to create her most progressive undertaking to date. The Village of Friendly Relations would become the signature identity of The Children's Country School.

The Village of Friendly Relations became necessary when the children of the school began growing vegetables haphazardly around campus along walkways, in the middle of manicured grass, and wherever children felt the impulse to throw seeds. As the vegetables grew, so did the frustration of Mary as children began to make borders around their new enterprises and became modern day squatters on campus.

Mary called the children together and gave an impromptu assembly about community and used John Dickinson's *The Liberty Song* as a teaching tool for "united we stand...divided we fall." Mary taught the children that a village that is interdependent of its members becomes a community. The idea of the Village of Friendly Relations was born in the imagination of Mary and through the eyes of eager, ambitious children.

The children decided that they needed a store to sell their vegetables. They asked Mary for wood to build a store. She replied that she needed her wood and was unable to give it to the children. However, she would provide them with the land on which to build. By brainstorming with the children, Mary taught them that if they went to a bank and applied for a loan, then they would be able to buy the wood needed to build their store. So, off trudged four little boys to the First National Bank of Los Gatos to get a loan to purchase wood to build their store. Mary made sure that the bank knew all about this enterprise by calling ahead and explaining the situation to the bank manager. Tom Watkins and Bill Yabroff, two of the boys who made that fateful trek into town, remember the meeting with the bank manager and signing all the papers necessary to get a loan. Tom recalls, "*It was quite exciting and memorable that these adults treated us so seriously.*"

The next lesson instilled by Mary was that of a mortgage and working capital. The children learned that they needed income to pay off this $100 mortgage and working capital to start their vegetable selling business. Mary helped with the working capital by listing jobs that needed to be completed on campus. These jobs included general cleaning inside and outside buildings, such as sweeping the tower steps, wiping dishes for two weeks consecutively (and being docked for failure to show up or breakage), and caring for the ponies by getting up at 6 a.m. every morning to curry, feed, water, and clean the corral. The salaries ranged from 15 cents to $2.00 a month. The highest salary went to the "poniers." Since the loan for the store was $100, then $15 working capital was needed to open the store. Employment Night was another name for pay day for these children who were pooling their income to get their Village off the ground.

Many assemblies were needed to help keep the children cohesive in their effort to build a community. Mary recites, "*All shut your eyes and in your mind locate a nice place, a right place, can you see the street with your stores?...I'm going to expect you to make your Village on paper by drawing it…now open your eyes.*" The houses would resemble English cottages like the ones that the children saw on their field trip to Carmel.

Village assembly topics included pioneering, corporation, interdependence, and government. Empowered children learned and explained after months of assembly discussions how they were pioneers who needed to be interdependent on each other to form their own government. It was during these assemblies that the children decided that their town would be named the Village of Friendly Relations with Friendly being the password for all members.

Montgomery Wards catalogs were studied and excursions to hardware stores and seeds stores were made by excited children. The children saw a need for more than just a store in their Village. There was need for a bank to hold their working capital, as well as to provide money for the children to buy the vegetables from the store. Allowances from parents to their children were deposited in the bank. A gift shop was needed to sell art work and crafts made in class. Added to the plans was a two story tea house where children would make tea on the ground floor and customers would go upstairs to drink tea and look out on their thriving Village.

The buildings would be distinctive in their design. The bank would have round windows like coins. The general store would have a protruding counter out the window for conducting transactions. The gift shop would have a half door to allow for friendly access to the Village shoppers. The tea room would include a giant handle on the side and a spout on top. The innocent imagination of the children breathed life and ownership into their village.

Building the General Store

Building the Gift Shop

Building the Village Bank

Two-story Tea House

Builders of the Newspaper Office

Writing Happy Times in the Newspaper Office

A newspaper office was needed to print their school newspaper, Happy Times. The newspaper office housed a mimeograph machine with the purple print and odor that only a student prior to the 1980's could describe. The newspaper was used as a tool for teachers to provide hands on lessons in grammar and writing. It was used by the students as a means of expressing themselves. Happy Times first issue was in June of 1938 and continued well into the late 1950's.

Happy Times was not written on a monthly basis, but rather according to the boarding school culture. Happy Times was threaded by common themes such as summer camp, Christmas, Easter, and graduation. The newspaper also sprang into circulation when their community was in need of a "special edition" like a fire on campus, a sundial being donated to the Village, or Miss Glassford's glasses being found by a Terrier who retrieved them to the local fire station. Whatever the occasion, Happy Times truly was a newspaper written by the children and for the children.

Each edition of Happy Times had a structure and familiarity to it. The staff of the newspaper would sometimes consist of as many as six editors: chief, literary, feature, news, sports, and art. The rest of the staff was made up of reporters. The chief editor was given an editor's page to write on such topics as “Don’t quit,” “Be truthful,” “Happiness is a must,” “What makes a good citizen?” and “Relax, not now America!” written at the end of WWII.

The literary editor printed poems written by children. The news editor reported on new students, campus pets, the garden, The Village, children at play, and lost & found. The sports editor was more loosely the “recess” or “free time” reporter describing games of kick the can, hide and go seek, and the latest tetherball champion.

True to the school’s artistic culture, the newspaper was adorned with drawings and sketches that danced on or near words along the pages. Many times the cover of Happy Times was enhanced with crayon markings to embolden the script. Poems were given drawings to enhance their meaning. Even the classifieds, yes, the newspaper had a classified section, were hand-drawn advertisements of local businesses such as, Carl Watts Wholesale Lumber, Templeman’s Hardware, Ballin’s Men & Boy’s Wear, and Margaret Burnham’s Cottage Candies. Each advertisement had its own unique script and drawing that only could have been created through a child’s imagination.

Happy Times cover

Happy Times cover

At the least, Happy Times, is a practical example of children practicing grammar and writing skills in a newspaper format. At the most, Happy Times is a living, breathing account of a boarding school community living through an adult world's Depression and soon-to-be World War, seen through the eyes of a child.

Mr. Toyon, an architect and friend of the school, assisted in the laying of foundations for the houses. The General Store has the etchings of the Village builders on the inside corner of its cement floor: T.W, I.Y., J.M., S.B. 5/19/38. A home movie taken of the campus in 1938 shows the children measuring, sawing, and hammering. Children saunter about their wood-framed structures like expectant parents deep in thought. This was not children at play, but rather children at work building their Village.

Mary writes, *"Their Village is progressing in amazing rapidity and much variety in overalled figures running to garden and lay brick at recess and after school*

Happy Times classifieds

times. It is quite thrilling to me to see the Village vegetable gardens produce a bit of the Sunday dinner. Even the Nursery children are drawing plans for the General Store, in which to sell the products of the Village. The children are making things in arts and crafts shop to sell for Christmas so they will have some money to help build more of the Village. Every night, when we aren't practicing for the Christmas musical, the boys are working away in the shop sawing, painting, weaving mats, and planning ahead."

As the Village became more than just an idea, a Village trademark was discussed and a contest for design was created. Tom Watkin's design was chosen and his beautiful interpretation is donned in crayon. Through the eyes of an eleven year old, Tom describes the trademark: *"the circle on which the houses are built indicate the world or eternity with no beginning and no end. The oats and wheat mean 'we shall have all our needs supplied and we shall not want.' In the center is a gate. This gate is never closed to friendly people. At the end of the path life, truth, and love await. We are surrounded by nature on all sides."*

The Village of Friendly Relation's trademark

The VOFR grew to include a circled brick pathway connecting the little houses. A lamp to provide light in the Village at night and a sun dial were donated with grand processions and speeches offered by the keepers of each house. The three foot rock tower on which the sun dial sat atop still stands at the NW corner of the Village. The bank issued its own check books and kept a ledger of Villagers' deposits, withdrawals and balances.

The newspaper became a source for Village affairs offering advice on the best crops to grow and how to figure interest on a 3 cent withdrawal from the bank. The children constructed their own Morse code system between buildings for communication. Bill Yabroff, store manager, would Morse code his brother, Irv, the bank manager, to check if a Village shopper had the funds needed to purchase an item in the store. Bill could never figure out Morse code, so instead he would stick his head out of the window and call to his brother. Bill states, *"She (Mary Orem) gave us a chance to build the Village....operate it...make all our own mistakes. I mean it was an incredible education."*

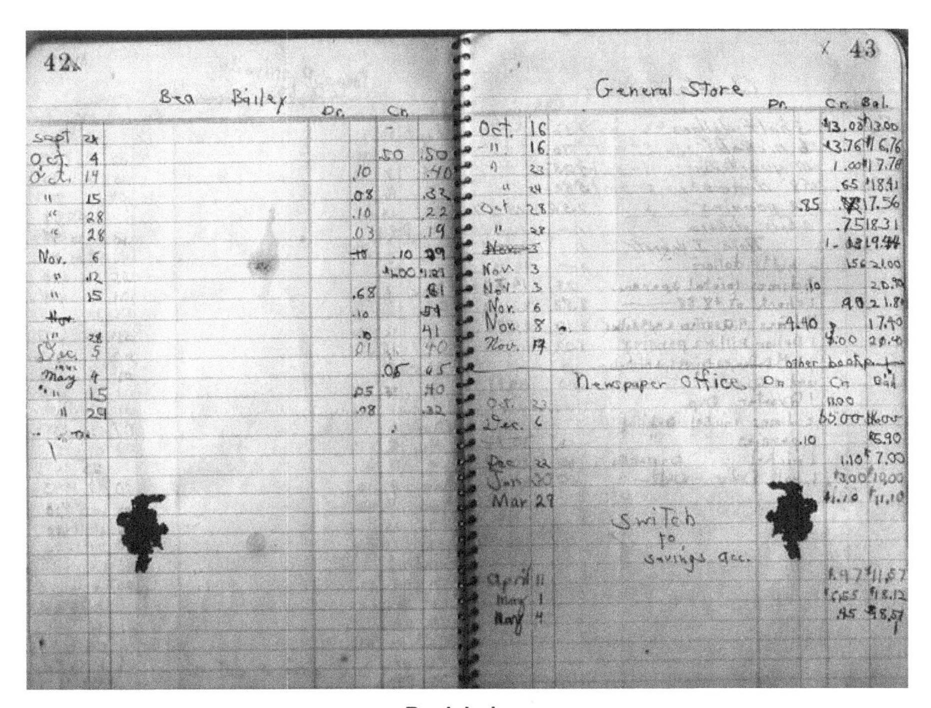

Bank ledger

No. $
194
TO
For

	Dollars	Cents
Amt. Fwd.		
Amt. Dep.		
Total		
Amt. Chgd.		
Bal. Fwd.		

Los Gatos 194 No.

Friendly Relations Village Bank

OF CHILDREN'S COUNTRY SCHOOL

PAY to the Order of $

DOLLARS

Bank checkbook

The Village Bank

The Village became known outside its invisible walls. Nearby schools took field trips to view the Village first hand. The September, 1939 edition of Sunset magazine dedicated a photo log to the Village. The photo log emphasizes that the schools of the West are trying to provide children "*the opportunity to put their academic knowledge to practical use...next step in this model community's development is to be the election of a Mayor. So far the young citizens have not found a candidate who measures up to their high ideals!*"[24]

VILLAGE OF FRIENDLY RELATIONS

SCHOOLS all over the West are beginning to apply the theory that in order for youngsters to really learn a subject, they must have the opportunity to put their academic knowledge to practical use. At The Children's Country School, near Los Gatos, Calif., for instance, the children are building a miniature town where they can apply the lessons taught in class. English composition, as an example, is put to practice in the tiny newspaper office they've built where the school paper is published.

Construction of the little buildings is done under the supervision of a Los Gatos contractor. Next step in this model community's development is to be the election of a mayor. So far the young citizens haven't found a candidate who measures up to their high ideals!

CARPENTER. He's putting finishing touches on the General Store where candy, shoe laces, etc. will be sold. The children named the model town "The Village of Friendly Relations." Architecture is Old English with fairy-tale influence

STUDYING BLUEPRINTS. All buildings are designed and constructed by the children and are 8-10 feet high

FEMININE BRICKLAYERS discuss the process of mixing cement. A real bank loan financed the whole project

CRAFTSMAN. Children learn the value of fine craftsmanship, and standards are high in Village of Friendly Relations

GIFT SHOP, where children's handicraft products will be sold. Parents are customers. Profits will pay off bank loan

TEA ROOM—only 2-story building in the community—where tea or luncheon can be served to visitors and parents

REWARD. Day's labor is over and food looks good to tired workmen. Landscaping the grounds will complete project

4

Sunset magazine September, 1939

Nathalie writes, "*We enrich the school subjects greatly and the 'learning by doing' idea is followed through in our Village of Friendly Relations which include the General Store, Newspaper, and Village meetings where the children discuss policies and problems according to democratic procedures. The nucleus of its activity is 'the community' where by living experiment the children face the fundamental problems of economics to ethics living together in a friendly cooperation. The fundamental rudiments of the 3 r's assume their rightful place in the importance of the curriculum and become interesting and necessary tools for the individual contribution to the Village idea. The workers of the Village Bank send the bankers back to the classroom demanding instruction in computing interest on making bank statements. The problems of the Chicken Coop send the children to lumber companies. with pad and pencil and yardstick. Problems of irrigation for the vegetables gardeners bring a demand for research in social science books about dams & waterways.*"

Though the Village of Friendly Relations was a children's place to live and learn, Mary was the puppet master carefully guiding the strings that orchestrated this magical endeavor. The records of the Village are so detailed and well-preserved. This was a practical experiment that Mary was conducting for an unknown educational institution.

In a letter dated September 22, 1937, Mary writes, "*I would like so much to discuss with you our plans for the possibilities of turning our school into an experimental plant for promoting Peace. I am sure, from all I know of you, that you will agree with us that training for Peace must begin with the young children. If a nation-wide educational program were planned and carried through in the various elementary schools, the next generation would not be so prone to follow the blare and threats of propagandists, because in their early learning, they had been given the chance to draw their own conclusions by the HONEST knowledge of how and why propaganda for war is started.*"

Mary's thesis is meticulously well-designed The purpose of the Village was three-fold: "*To salvage at an early age the child of superior abilities whose talents in the usual group situation might be lost to society...to bring to the child a way of education that is practical and applicable to his adult life...to develop a stability by offering opportunities to adjust to his own age group in society, before going out into a chaotic and changing world.*"

Mary drew from her Wheelock training by instilling her 'Rules for Guidance of the Young Child in the Village:'

Teacher with children in front of the General Store

Girl Scouts in front of Gift Shop

Builders of the General Store

General Store with Tower in the background

Two-story Tea House

"Training for peace must begin in the nursery, where tolerance and a willingness to share are natural growths in adjustment...to discard the chaff before prejudice has a chance to set in...that friendly settling of disagreements is possible in a group of variegated backgrounds and so through understanding and working for a common good, Peace is possible.

To give reason for learning, and learning's relativity to life by practical experiment...to offer opportunities to experiment with many kinds of materials until he finds his particular bent or interest and to open the way for him to develop that bent without fear or self consciousness and no thing will keep him from the attainment of knowledge. For as the twig is bent, the tree inclines."

Mary designed her Rules for the Village with clear understanding and influence from both Alfred Adler and Jane Addams and their ideals of social democracy:

"In our Village each business is run for the good of the whole Village. There are rules which keep the separate businesses in line for the best interests of the whole Village. There is a central government which is made for the good of everyone and it has rules about how a co-operative should work.

Like our National government, the Village has a Democratic form of government, For the Villagers; By the Villagers; and From the Villagers. Then, the majority vote rules, and obedience to rules made for the good of everyone leads to harmony and friendly relations. This is what our Village stands for."

Future guidelines were addressed so that original Village ideals would not be compromised:

"All gifts of money for the Village shall go into the scholarship fund to be used for children who otherwise would not have the opportunity to participate in this way of Learning by Doing - Building for Citizenship by real experiment in their own Village of Friendly Relations, and to participate in the Village is opening the door an entering a Child's Paradise, where the goal is towards successful adult living and leadership in his community.

No gifts shall be used for furthering the Village buildings, businesses or improvements. Our Village must earn its way in order that the children will continue to have the opportunity to learn by experiment in a true and real situation.

All articles for sale in the Village must be approved by the Director of our school, after the approval of the Village. Each business will have a model of it's building to be used as a Bank and our friends will have the privilege of contributing to our scholarship fund as a material expression of their sincere approval of the aims and ideals of the Village of Friendly Relations.

Each business will keep strict account of its earning in a Village ledger, and at the end of each working day, hand it, with the money of the day, into the Bank.

Each business will help he building of the Village as a whole; roads will be needed, lamps to light the paths, gardens, a railroad will be built; all of these are called Improvements. The way the Improvements are paid for, is by each one paying a certain amount to the Village. This is called a Tax.

Each business will pay a Tax for the benefit of making a beautiful and useful unit of the Village. The Tax is measured by the amount of money each business will make after the expenses are paid."

The expansion of the Village was in the planning stage. A Library would serve for lending and buying books, as well as for future magazine subscriptions. A Floral Shop would be adorned with flowers and potted plants from the children's gardens with singing canaries in cages through out the shop. The Tea Room could be reserved for birthday parties and special occasions. Bakery goods to be sold in the Tea Room would be baked in the

VILLAGE RULES

Our Mother School is organized as a Co-Operative; that is, each head of a department, has his own little school or business and runs it to the best of his abilities for the good of everyone in the whole Co-Operative.

Then, there is a central government which is made for the good of everyone and it has rules about how the CO-Operative should work.

So, in our Village each business is run for the good of the whole Village. There are rules which keep the separate businesses in line for the best interests of the whole Village.

Like our national government, the Village has a Democratic form of government; For the Villagers, By the Villagers, and From the Villagers. Then, the majority vote rules, and Ovedience to rules made for the good of everyone leads to Harmony and Friendly Relations. This is what our Village stands for.

Mary Orem's Village Rules

Village Possibilities

Each business will have its special purpose.

Each business will help the building of the Village as a whole; that is, roads will be needed, lamps to light the paths, gardens, a railroad will be built; all of these are called Improvements. The way the Improvements are paid for, is by each one paying a certain amount to the Village. This is called a Tax.

Each business will pay a Tax for the benefit of making a beautiful and useful unit of the Village. The Tax is measured by the amount of money each business will make after the expenses are paid.

Mary Orem's Village Possibilities

school kitchen. A Post Office would sell school stationary, picture post cards, and Village stamps commemorating historical occasions. The General Store would focus its inventory more on Villager's necessities such as Kleenex, toothpaste, pencils, shoelaces, and flashlights. A Town Hall would be used for puppet shows and showing of movies. The Town Hall would be constructed in the middle of the Village to symbolize togetherness.

Unfortunately, the times were not favorable for expansion in the Village. The events at Pearl Harbor would bring an end to Village growth. The monies planned for the expanding Village were needed more in the daily operations of the school. The Village was put on hold indefinitely, as was the nation.

On the brink of World War II, the Village of Friendly Relations was not only relevant, but necessary. Mary writes, "*The Village of Friendly Relations will typify the City of Tomorrow for the children, who will one day take their places in communities over the country...the laws and rules for living together will be worked out by the children themselves by trial and error. Our toys are constructive and censored; no miniature tools of destruction. Our password is friendliness, our weapon is reason, and our goal is to develop leaders for Peace.*"

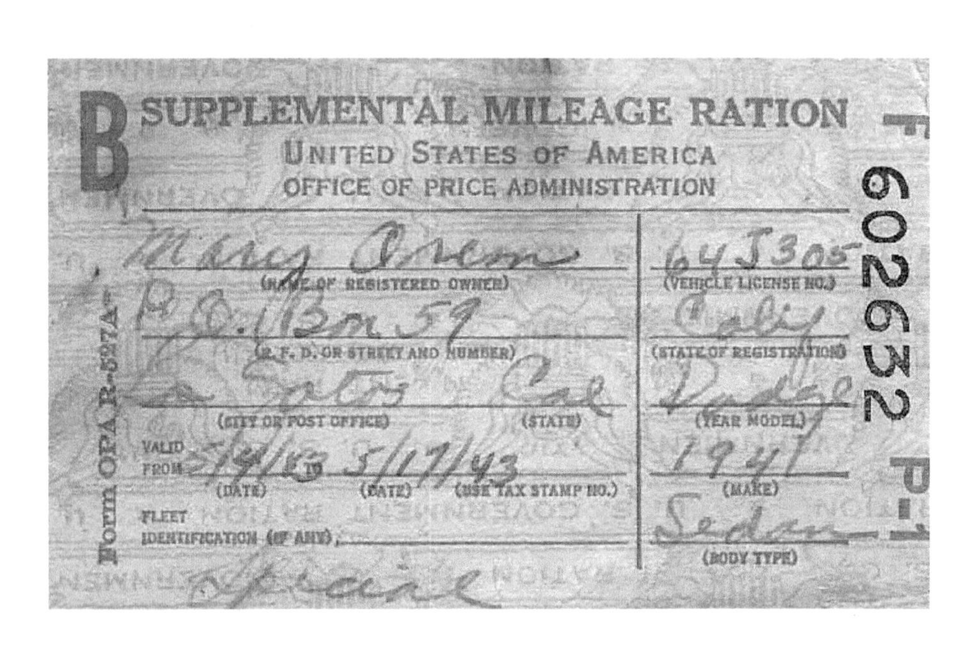

B SUPPLEMENTAL MILEAGE RATION

UNITED STATES OF AMERICA

OFFICE OF PRICE ADMINISTRATION

F 602632 P-1

Form OPA R-537A

(NAME OF REGISTERED OWNER)	64J305 (VEHICLE LICENSE NO.)
P.O. Box 59 (R. F. D. OR STREET AND NUMBER)	Calif (STATE OF REGISTRATION)
(CITY OR POST OFFICE) (STATE)	Dodge (YEAR MODEL)
VALID FROM (DATE) TO 5/17/43 (DATE) (USE TAX STAMP NO.)	1941 (MAKE)
FLEET IDENTIFICATION (IF ANY)	Sedan (BODY TYPE)

CHAPTER 8

THE WAR YEARS

"Californians can truly say 'that which we feared has come upon us'. The ghastly affair at Honolulu struck me so hard that for two days I suffered from shock. The scars of war are so deep and horrible that it seems as though Nature herself would rebel and allow at least one generation of children to grow to old age in peace."

~TCCS Parent

TCCS had withstood the trials of the Depression era and the struggles of pioneering a new school in uncertain times. Their Village of Friendly Relations was thriving and in full operation. Their world-renown Pied Piper's Call summer camp was consistently attracting over double its student body in numbers of campers. As their student body and infrastructure began to expand and grow, the school was beginning to stand on solid ground. A ground that had overnight become shaky for an entire country.

The initial reaction by Mary to the Pearl Harbor attack was for the safety of her children. She immediately took action in making sure that her location was safe. In a letter dated December 9, 1941, she writes, "*Since Sunday, the emergency of war plans has arisen and I do want to talk with you. As far as we are situated here at school the country seems rather safe for the present. However, we are investigating as fast as possible the possibility of moving the school en masse into Arizona perhaps or some recommended area where the danger is more remote. The school is situated in the foothills, away from the main highways and is not conspicuous as we have simple low buildings rather spread out…have you still a ranch, and if so, what chance would there be for working out some plan on a percentage basis whereby I could bring say fifty children and staff. I would like to know in case of the need for sudden evacuation.*"

After the initial shock of war, Nathalie corresponds with parents in letters dated December 14th, "*...our routine has taken shape again. The first few days of the War, after the first shock made all of us take stock of the situation from all possible angles...After the first upsetting news of the war and our inquiries about safety of location, we have now been assured that we are very well situated away from vital centers. In fact, half of the school is remaining for the holiday rather than go to the cities.*"

December
14,
1941.

Dear Mr. andMrs. Dayton:

Benton left yesterday morning and I trust he arrived safely in the south. We were very glad that he was to have the opportunity to go to see his grandmother.

After the first upsetting news ofthe war and our inquiries about safety of location we have now been assured that we are very well situated away from vital centers. In fact, half of the school is remaining for the holiday rather than go to the cities.

I know that Benton will have a lovely time. Please accept our very best wishes for a happy holiday time.

Sincerely,
Nathalie Yakoff
Secretary.

Parent letter following Pearl Harbor attack

TCCS would become a haven in a time of war for many families. New children were added to the student body by families that now had a military personnel or wife who was no longer a stay at home mother. Nathalie embraces the new direction of the school by writing, *"There is great need for places where tiny children and young babies may be placed; where the atmosphere is that of love and lack of fear; where the roots of a higher law may take hold in baby thought. So the school is rededicating its service to children. Its staff of loving and trained 'mothers' stand ready for direction."*

The 1941 Pied Piper's Call would be the largest to date. Nathalie writes, *"We had instead of the 75 children we had set the limit on, 120 children. The need was so great that we just were unable to refuse and be patriotic in this emergency when children are left out of the great national war program and so desperately need a place to learn to be good citizens. We had resident children from all over during the war years. New Zealand, India, a little boy whose father was the Ambassador of South America, Sumatra, Dutch, English. We had just a fascinating group."*

By 1944, the Los Gatos Times reported that more than 500 Los Gatos High School graduates were serving in the war. Headlines in the Times bellowed 'Yoo-Hoo The Boys And Be Proud Of It,' 'Seeing The Boys Off To Camp' and 'Townfolk Urged to Open Homes to Soldiers.'[25] The Children's Country School did its part by adding families of military persuasion, as well as staff and children from abroad. Two displaced Jewish teachers came to teach middle school and music. John Brady, a ten year old resident student, remembers these new teachers as being so enthusiastic and grateful to be a part of the school.

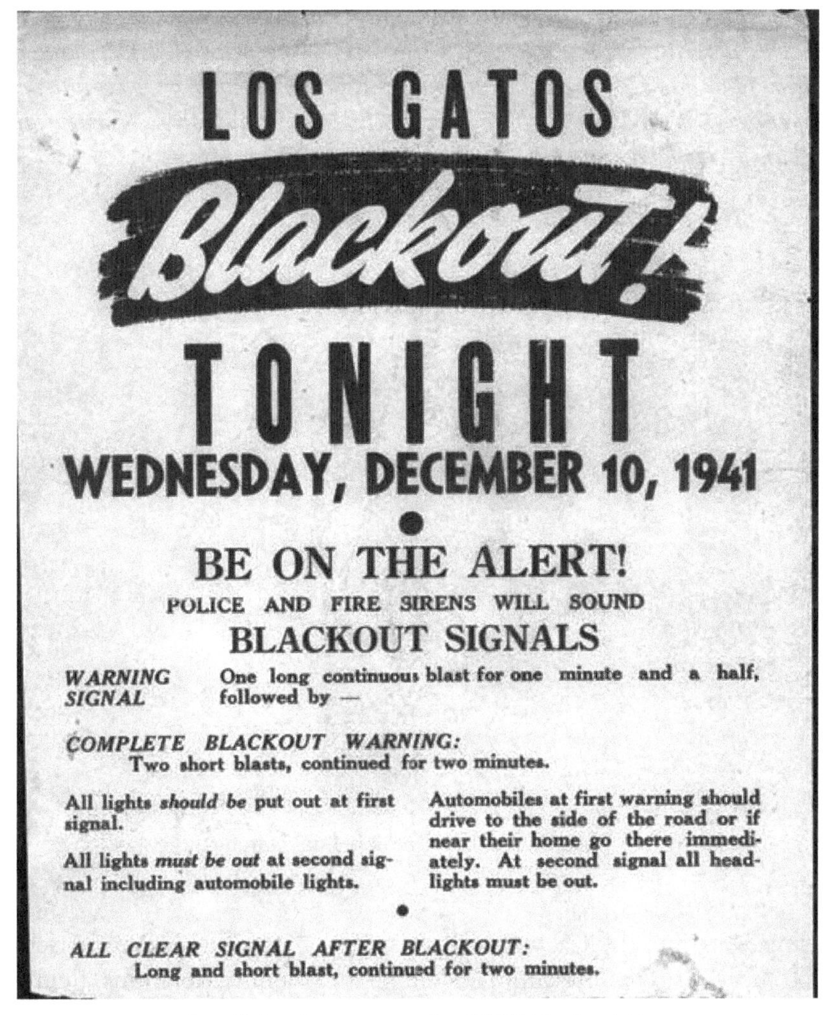

Los Gatos town poster for WWII blackouts[26]

These uncertain times would also cause added stress to TCCS' beloved house mother, Miss Saki. With the country setting of the school, Miss Saki was somewhat hidden from public view and the public requirement to report for Japanese internment. Jan Hill remembers playing hide and go seek with Miss Saki when visitors came on campus. Jack Watkins, also a resident student, remembers Saki lying on the floorboards of the station wagon when they drove into Los Gatos. Both children at the time just thought of these episodes as hide and go seek games with no grave consequences.

Bill Yabroff remembers *"the sad day she left, she was crying. She hugged everyone of us."* Nathalie describes Saki's eventual fate during the war: *"Miss Saki took three children with her to Washoe Nevada: Ron Hill, Ann Marie Shultz and Marty Schultz. This arrangement lasted only from March to June of 1942. Saki then was moved to Tule Lake which she hated. She petitioned Department of Interior to be allowed to move to an Indian Reservation which was granted. She spent the rest of the War teaching Navajo children."* Saki adds, *"I was grateful for that. I felt no bitterness."*

Miss Saki at Los Gatos holiday parade

During wartime, TCCS would lose some of its progressive curriculum due to necessity for survival. The Village of Friendly Relations, field trips to San Francisco, and annual summer treks to Lake Tahoe and the school's

Rio Del Mar beach house all took a back seat to war time rationing. Requests by TCCS to receive the gas rationing needed to make such trips were met with disapproval. A reply letter from the Office of Defense Transportation & Emergency Management states: "*We have decided that we cannot authorize trips of this length especially for children who are now located in a summer camp in an excellent camping locality such as yours.*"

Not only was it difficult for TCCS to travel, but it also became difficult for them to get their usual amount of supplies delivered to their campus. Nathalie explains that "*tire and gas rationing, curtailed train, bus & plane service, with preference given to official Government travel is making parents, as well as ourselves, realize the acuteness of the times. Last week on a contact trip to Vallejo, barrage balloons hung continually over the town.*"

Food rationing would play a major role in the daily livelihood of the boarding school. Each child was required to provide 1 ½ lbs. of sugar for school-wide meals. This amount of sugar would soon grow inadequate to the demand. Nathalie writes to a parent, "*The question of sugar is becoming something of a major problem here. If you have used Margaret's stamp for the January-April period, would you please send along the stamp for the next period. One stamp or five pounds will just cover the one term. If you have any sugar on hand and wish to send along sugar instead that would be fine.*"

The students soon became aware of the scarcity of food. Dean Eyre, a 7 year old at the time, remembers throwing food under the table at a meal and being told, "don't you know there's a war on?" Many kids remember the basic food principle of the time: 'if you take it, you eat it.' The school bought a cow, Blossom, to provide milk at meals and the children's vegetable garden earned a more regal title of Victory Garden.

On the home front, the call came to buy war bonds; for gas and food rationing; for scrap drives; for women's silk and nylon hosiery and for local volunteers to help harvest the prune crops with so many ranchers away from home. Yehudi Menuhin performed a private concert on campus to raise money for the school.

Gas rationing would prove to have a profound effect on the entire school community. Parents, especially those who lived out of state, found it increasingly difficult to afford the trip to Los Gatos to visit their children. The following letter became a common theme in correspondence with the school. A parent writes, "*I am so sorry that I could not get down there by today, as I'd hoped until the last moment, but I have not yet got the gas rationing to*

The children's Victory Garden

UNITED STATES OF AMERICA
OFFICE OF PRICE ADMINISTRATION

394107 EE

WAR RATION BOOK No. 3

Void if altered

NOT VALID WITHOUT STAMP

Identification of person to whom issued: PRINT IN FULL

Mary Orem

(First name) (Middle name) (Last name)

Street number or rural route

City or post office State

AGE	SEX	WEIGHT Lbs.	HEIGHT Ft. In.	OCCUPATION

SIGNATURE Mary Orem
(Person to whom book is issued. If such person is unable to sign because of age or incapacity, another may sign in his behalf.)

WARNING
This book is the property of the United States Government. It is unlawful to sell it to any other person, or to use it or permit anyone else to use it, except to obtain rationed goods in accordance with regulations of the Office of Price Administration. Any person who finds a lost War Ration Book must return it to the War Price and Rationing Board which issued it. Persons who violate rationing regulations are subject to $10,000 fine or imprisonment, or both.

OPA Form No. R-130

LOCAL BOARD ACTION

Issued by (Local board number) (Date)

Street address

City State

Book X issued

(Signature of issuing officer)

War ration card

make the move and I applied for the gas two weeks ago." In this letter, a soldier father writes to his son, "*Daddy won't be able to get back for awhile now. I wish that I could see you. You must be a great big boy and very strong by now. Don't forget to be a good boy and remember that daddy is thinking of you and hoping to get back to you as soon as he can.*"

IMPORTANT INSTRUCTIONS

1. Coupons can be used only in connection with the vehicle described on the front cover. Detached coupons are VOID.
2. If you stop using your car, this book and all unused coupons must be surrendered to your Board within 5 days.
3. If you sell your car, this book and all unused coupons must be surrendered to your Board. The purchaser will not be issued a gasoline ration unless he presents the receipt which you receive at the time of such surrender.

FOLD HERE

A BASIC MILEAGE RATION
UNITED STATES OF AMERICA
OFFICE OF PRICE ADMINISTRATION

NAME OF REGISTERED OWNER
ADDRESS—NUMBER AND STREET
CITY AND STATE
LICENSE No. AND STATE | YEAR MODEL AND MAKE

Holder must fill in any blank spaces above before the first purchase of gasoline.

941008

OPA FORM R-525 C — A — A17 — MILEAGE — 941008 — (License No.) (State)

Gas ration stamps

O. P. A. Form No. R-306
Serial No. C28779628
UNITED STATES OF AMERICA
OFFICE OF PRICE ADMINISTRATION
SUGAR PURCHASE CERTIFICATE
Not Valid Before 8/11/42 Date
DUPLICATE

THIS IS TO CERTIFY THAT:
Name The Children's Country School Address: Kennedy Rd.
City: Los Gatos County: Santa Clara State: Calif.
is authorized to accept delivery of
One Hundred (100) pounds of sugar pursuant to Rationing Order No. 3 (Sugar Rationing Regulations) of, and at a price not to exceed the maximum price established by the Office of Price Administration.

Date August 11, 1942
Local Rationing Board No. 43-1
By [signature] Signature of issuing officer
Santa Clara (County) Calif. (State) Deputy Registrar (Title)
To be retained by Local Rationing Board.

Sugar purchase certificate

John Brady remembers that parents were so rare on campus that when they came you showed them off like trophies. The parents who visited campus acted as surrogate parents for other children by mingling more than usual with children craving for attention.

TCCS would become a permanent home for many of the children for the next four years. A bittersweet photo exists of over 25 children dressed in fine attire singing carols in the auditorium. The date on the photograph is Dec. 24, 1945. A campus that was virtually empty during holidays was now almost full with children. These four years of virtual isolation from parents proves why these grown-children of today still have such a close bond with the school, and more importantly, with each other.

Thanksgiving during the war years

Although times were trying, Mary used the War as a means of initiating new curriculum. TCCS started a Works Program for the children. Taps was played at 6:15am rising and again at 8:15 pm for all quiet at night. The children could earn Victory pins for mopping floors, painting fences, and cleaning buildings. Some children were even driven to

Children in the auditorium on December 24, 1945

nearby ranches to help pick fruit. Nathalie corresponds to a parent, "*Noel is fine and becoming such a young lady. She won her first V-pin for good work well done on the Work Program that we have. Only very few children so far have won the coveted award and Noel is the only girl to wear one. We're very proud of her.*"

The school went outside it's own community to immerse the children in the larger world. In 1945, representatives of 50 countries met in San Francisco at the United Nations Conference to draw up the United Nations Charter. The Children's Country School was represented at the meeting, as well. Jan Hill describes the scene. "*If you say anything at all about her (Mary Orem) you got to say the woman had connections. We saw the forming of the United Nations at San Francisco Opera House. We got to see all the dignitaries from all the countries. I knew that was a thrilling moment. I think we all knew that.*"

Brian Epps recalls that eventful day "*we went all over gathering autographs from all the delegates from all the different countries. That whole depth of experience opened up a lot for me. She opened my awareness to being intellectually curious about things. I'm sure that if it had not been for her, my life would have been drastically different*".

The Pied Piper's Call summer camp also adopted the Works Program placing children into their usual age groups with names more indicative of the times such as the The Dauntless Marines, The Dawn Patrol, The Sturdy WAACS, and The Little Sailors. Campers were given "night watch" duties to make sure no lights, including flashlights from sleeping tents, shone after 8:15pm. Impromptu air raid drills were conducted at night on campus. Jan Hill recalls having to run with her blanket to the cement wall that divided the upper field and the basketball courts. She remembers taking it very seriously and having to lie down as flat as possible without making a sound until a "big kid" gave the all clear call.

The Sturdy WAACS

In April of 1945, the death of Franklin Roosevelt was a momentous day on campus. Children remember an assembly in the morning to announce his death and the rest of the day was dedicated to children remembering their President by writing a poem or letter or drawing a picture. Students were encouraged to go out on campus and find a place to reflect. Later that afternoon, the children gathered again to share their reflections. Their pieces of work were bound together into a book and sent to Eleanor Roosevelt. Months later, a hand-written thank you letter was delivered to the school with Eleanor Roosevelt's signature.

True to her progressive nature, Mary attended an unknown conference five weeks after the attack on Pearl Harbor. It was at this conference that she developed a strategic plan for guiding the school through war time. The main focus of Mary's strategy was summed up as *"School must aid in every way in the war effort."*

TCCS was fulfilling its wartime strategic plan of 'aiding in the war effort' in a variety of ways. The school's summer camp allowed for 120 children when it planned for only 75 campers. It issued a Works Program that benefited the children and the surrounding community. A Victory Garden symbolized hope and V-pins demonstrated the concept of citizenship. Displaced Jewish teachers were hired by the school and the school community adopted a family in Holland and one in Czechoslovakia to send boxed food. A group of 12 boys lead by 13 year old Bill Yabroff, were given a shack work station for storing and drying picked apricots that would be donated to the army. Even one of the school's horses, MacArthur, was donated to the war effort. TCCS became the surrogate family to many children whose parents were busy aiding in the war effort themselves. And when Franklin Roosevelt passed away, TCCS consoled their country's first lady with hand-made offerings that could only be created with a child's sincerity.

Children drying apricots

Mary's strategic plan for the school during the war years was put into practice by dedicated teachers. The teachers were given guidelines by Mary to follow for executing her principles. She emphasized that teachers must be a model for children by always showing good character. For Mary writes, *"Our way of life must be kept in tact by producing children with good character."* This would be accomplished by protecting children from war hysteria and possible emergency preparations by carrying on normal tasks. Mary believed that the purpose of educators during the war was to be *"defenders and practitioners of democracy."*

Mary believed that the children were the future defenders of democracy in a world that might not be as free in post-war. She wanted to instill the qualities of a nation in a school setting first so that these children would continue these ideals in the future. Mary wanted to express 'world citizenship' through activity such as the school sponsoring a European family in need. She wanted to *"teach hatred of evil…not hatred of evil doers."* This was accomplished by having lessons from a child's point of view turning the topic of 'evil' into one of 'unfair,' 'cheating,' and 'falseness.'

Mary Orem's WWII strategic teaching plan for 'world citizenship'

Mary wanted the topic of democracy to be one of learning by doing. It was already put into effect with the Village of Friendly Relations where children had been creating and enforcing their own rules and laws prior to the outbreak of war. She now wanted to create a "*greater emotional appeal in teaching democracy*" through dramatization.

This was accomplished by having the children learn and perform the Ballad for Americans. Paul Robeson, who recorded this anthem, had visited and performed on campus years earlier. Bob Klang, a 10 year old student at the time, remembers vividly this experience and how it still resonates with him today. He explains, "*They taught that to us. It glorified democracy. It glorified equality. We were all one people. It didn't matter what our color was. It didn't matter what our name was. It didn't matter what our background was. We are Americans and this is a free country and it's a democratic country and everyone is respected and that was the message that we got.*"

Mary provided a school that refused to be stagnant in a turbulent time. She continued to persevere and teach the whole child in accordance to the world situation. Her dedication and the parents' confidence in her care is shown in a letter dated Aug. 14, 1944, by a Navy parent wanting to place his 4 ½ year old son at TCCS. He writes, "*The atmosphere of love and adherence to principle which motivates your school is exactly what is needed in these times of confusion. The rush to give a young boy the proper foundation for a future life of usefulness on the side of Good in a world deeply in need of such activity. We do not underestimate the fine care and training and are deeply grateful for it.*"

Feb. 1st - New Term Begins -
aim = to reap the benefits of
building up of all the interests &
enthusiasm & to complete some
of our projects
"Chil. shud have feeling of relation
ship to their country & world -
ap apprec. of th Contrib. of
the past & a responsib.
Towards the future - Bit
of an idea of the fun of
work & abil. to carry thru
to completion abil. to adjust
in a changing system & not
have xper. of the jobless -
maladjusted failure - a rich
background of cultural things

Mary Orem's notes for teaching students during the war years

CHAPTER 9

TCCS, INC

"We are going to take all our dividends out in the intelligence of our children."

~Ralph Elsman

In October of 1945, the four founders initiated a new venture that would change the direction of the school. An advisory committee was organized to explore the possibility of the school becoming a corporation. The committee consisted of parents as well as Senator Sanborn Young and TCCS' next door neighbor and president of San Jose Water Company, Ralph Elsman. These two men advised the four partners to *"keep it simple, keep it within, don't let outsiders come in or you'll lose your personality. You'll lose what you started."*

Nathalie explains, *"The school is going into a non-profit corporation, which means that the four of us are relinquishing our ownership in the school and going on salary like the other teachers, in order that the school may be an established institution. We've worked hard to establish something fine and now we have to release it, just like raising a child and then when it's old enough to stand on its own feet, it has to be released."*

At the time of the incorporation, the four partners took a promissory note for $25,000 in lieu of a salary which none had received during the 10 years prior. This figure was divided evenly among the four partners: Mary Orem, Nathalie Wollin, Elizabeth Glassford, and Ann Boge.

It was also at this time that the tenets of the school were written. The tenets were based on the school motto 'as the twig is bent, the tree will grow.' The 'roots' of the tree were a country setting of contact with soil and children thinking outside of self. The 'trunk' of the tree was teaching basic values of respect for learning by doing, as well as joy of experience in a task well done. This would be best accomplished by keeping learning groups small enough to allow for individual expression. The 'leaves' of the tree are for the healing of the Nations.

Country School Files Articles of Incorporation

Articles of incorporation have been filed by the Children's Country School on Kennedy road, Los Gatos, Secretary of State Frank Jordan has revealed.

Listed as directors are Mary E. Orem, Elizabeth Glassford, Nathalie Yabroff, Ann M. Boge, all of Route 3, Box 13; Clara Edwards, Fairway Drive and McKee Road and Eleanor M. Brown, 1000 San Jose-Los Gatos Road. Leland H. Walker, with offices in the First National Bank Building, San Jose, was attorney for the corporation.

Newspaper clipping of TCCS becoming Incorporated

Children of all creeds would be learning to live together in mutual understanding and respect which would then lay the foundation for international understanding. TCCS was dubbed 'God's School.' The four founders dedicated it as so in the beginning and they believed that it would serve as a perpetual guide for its leaders.

The tenets encouraged that girls and boys should be brought up together in understanding and respect with all children having equal opportunity in all curriculum subjects. This would act as a prelude for men and women living together in community and family life. Lastly, the tenets promoted a 'different way of education' in which a superior child develops in a proper situation and setting for learning. An enriched school program would produce a well-rounded individual.

On January 2, 1946, the first meeting of the Board of Directors was called to order. At this meeting were all four partners. Mary Orem was unanimously elected president of the Board. Ann Boge was elected vice-president. Nathalie Wollin was elected secretary. The school tenets were then read and approved. The meeting was adjourned with Mary expressing her thanks for the trust put in her by the Board of Directors in electing her its first president.

CHAPTER 10

THE BIG HOUSE

"Calm is the main thing I remember. It was a remarkable atmosphere. The trust was just about total."

~John Brady, TCCS student

With the struggles of the war years beginning to dissipate, The Children's Country School was able to again breathe a sigh of relief that their doors were still open. The school was freshly incorporated. Good news abounded with the highlight being the soon-to-be return of Miss Saki from her wartime internment in Arizona. Saki said after the welcome back party given in her honor, *"I felt right at home."*

TCCS was just 8 months removed from D-Day and 24 hours removed from its first ever Board of Directors meeting. The resident children were sound asleep on a cold evening in January. The school was at peace. A peace that would be broken in alarming fashion.

Irving Yabroff, Nathalie's 20 year old son, was doing his laundry when he saw smoke coming from the basement of the Big House shortly after 10pm. He ran inside the Big House and told Aunt Ann, the house mother, to evacuate the children. *"I was sitting in bed reading,"* recalled Aunt Ann, *"then I heard a crackling sound, then I smelled smoke. Immediately, I went to the nursery, smoke was coming into it quite rapidly...and began pulling sleeping little babies out of bed. I had about five babies on the first trip."*

The Big House

Mr. Tallion (school architect) recounts that *"Miss Glassford phoned me about 10 o'clock." She said 'I think we have a fire over here.' I got dressed and got over so fast it seemed like only a few minutes."*

"I arrived at TCCS while the fire was well underway," recalled the school doctor, Horace Jones. *"The little children who had been evacuated from the burning building were lying on the floor covered with blankets, in front of a large open fire. No one showed any indication of fright or terror. All was calm and serene."* Another teacher recounts, *"They didn't look at all frightened…it was remarkable at how well trained they had been and how they went out of the burning house calmly and orderly."*

Dean Jennings, a junior high student, recalls, *"I was in the tent asleep when I awoke to find a group of boys waiting patiently for a place to sleep. I asked one of them what had happened and he replied 'the Big House is burning down.' I tried to listen for some sign of excitement…I found that most of the senior department was not aware that anything was happening. They were fast asleep in bed (outdoor tents)…not until morning did they learn that the Big House had been burned."*

Pete Haggard had driven to the school to visit his mother who was a teacher at the school. Haggard's account of the fire is vividly real. *"The smoke was so thick I could hardly see. Then I ran through the house to see if there were any children left in the house; there were not. One of the Yabroff boys and I tried to get the water hose hooked up, but the hose broke off and we couldn't get it to work. We ran to the back of the house and saw flames in the basement. I took some wood boxes and broke the window in. They got me two fire extinguishers. I emptied those on the fire. Mr. Tallion came and got some garden hose. The fire truck soon ran out of water. We used the garden hose while the truck was getting hooked up to the swimming pool. I saw then that the next house was going to catch on fire. I took off my shirt and wet it and wrapped it around my head. Then, I turned the hose on myself and wet my clothing and then turned the hose on the next house. I kept the top and sides next to the Big House wet. Mother was screaming for me to come away from the fire. I just knew that the house would start blazing all over if I didn't stay with it. The Fire Department soon got hooked up. I moved farther away, then I began to freeze in those wet clothes. It was sure hot close to that fire though. I think I had to keep the hose on myself as much as I did the house."*

About 10:45pm, next door neighbor Ralph Elsman, went over to the school and connected his hose. Elsman had his wife call PG&E to turn off the gas at the school. By this time, the house had caved in except for the north wall. Elsman explains, *"I pushed the pipes in with a pruning pole so they could not fall on any of the men. My clothes had caught on fire three or four times, so I went home at 12:45 am to put dry clothes on."*

The Elsmans housed children that night in their home. Mrs. Elsman exclaimed, *"I never knew such quiet children in all my life. It is not often that a fire is as orderly as that one was."* The Elsmans would end up lending the use of their guest house as a temporary school dormitory for the next six months.

Three fire engines fought the blaze that lasted some 2 ½ hours. There was confusion at first in locating the fire. Nathalie explains *"because the fire department was from Alma and they thought (TCCS) was at the top of the hill and it took 40 minutes for them to go up and come back to us. The Red Cross came and gave us blankets and took care of us. The house was lost, but we saved the nursery. We were so grateful that every child was safely evacuated from the building in less than six minutes that we have no room for regret at the loss of building and equipment."*

John Brady sums up the atmosphere from a child's perspective. He was sleeping on the front porch of the house that night. He recalls being awakened by adults to put on his bathrobe and directed towards the Village Of Friendly Relations where the children sang songs and ate sandwiches that night. He was eventually sent over the bridge to sleep at the Sara Heavenrich Cottage.

In the Los Gatos Times, the front page headlines exclaimed 'Children's Country School is Heavily Hit By Big Night Fire.' The February 12, 1946, Happy Times is now a historical document for the school with page after page dedicated to interviews with teachers, children, parents, firemen, and doctors giving detailed accounts of the Big House fire.

Housemother Aunt Ann lost all her belongings and Miss Saki was left with only a tea cup and golf clubs. In a letter to a parent two weeks following the fire, Nathalie writes, *"I am sorry to be so long in getting word to you about Henry's things, but this has been a hectic time for us. All of Henry's bedding, sheets, pad, rubber sheet, blankets and spread were burned. His rain outfit, all shoes, bathrobe, and slippers. All his socks and underwear, sweaters and corduroy jumpers. I was able to find two jumpers for him, a windbreaker and coveralls. In the meantime, he is warm in borrowed blankets. I was also able to fit him in new warm pajamas that came in so he is all right there."*

Children's Country School
Kennedy Road

ATOS TIMES

Los Gatos
Saratoga

...thills Overlooking the Famous Santa Clara Valley in the Heart of California

...S, CALIFORNIA FRIDAY, JANUARY 5, 1945 Twelve Pages No. 15

Children's Country School Is Heavily Hit By Big Night Fire

Express Gratitude

We wish to express our appreciation for the very fine work of the Alma and Almaden fire departments and the volunteer boys and their handling of the fire so that it did not spread; to our neighbors and friends in Los Gatos and San Jose for their generous offer of shelter and clothing; to the staff of the sheriff's office for their help; to the parents and teachers of the school family, for the calm and expert handling of the emergency situation.

Our gratitude to all of you.

CHILDREN'S COUNTRY SCHOOL

NEWS BRIEFS

LT. SEWALL (LAD) BROWN USN arrived in Los Gatos New Year's eve after serving for 21

TO FURTHER PLANS FOR VET MEMORIAL AT MEET TONIGHT

Steps to consolidate plans for securing a district memorial building honoring the men and women who have made the supreme sacrifice in the service of their country at war, will be taken tonight at a meeting called at the town hall at 7:30 o'clock.

For the past few months Col. E. H. Melvin has been appearing before various civic and fraternal

Italians In U. S. Uniforms To Visit Here Jan. 6 to 8

Major John I. Ferguson of the Ninth Service Command at Camp Roberts, California, has notified The Times and requested an announcement that three Italians, presumably former prisoners of war, will visit Los Gatos from Saturday to Monday in company with a U.S. Army enlisted man. The major's communication was as follows:

"This is to inform you, as required by War Department regulations, that three Italians will visit Los Gatos from January 6, 1945, to January 8, 1945. These Italians will be accompanied by one U.S. Army

Children All Safely Evacuated

Authorities of the Children's Country School on Kennedy road were chiefly concerned yesterday with the comfort and care of the 33 children who were burned out of their living quarters in the disastrous fire Wednesday night that entirely destroyed the Happy Parker House and all furnishings and belongings.

Happy Parker House, a two-story dwelling, composed the sleeping quarters of 20 of the 70 boarding children pupils, the nursery class room and part of the music class room. Everything

Front page article of fire in Los Gatos Times[27]

Chimney and ashes from Big House fire

STARK REMINDER—All that remains of the dormitory-classroom structure burned at the Children's Country Day School fire from which 25 children were saved is brick chimney, rising through the smoke. In lower picture, a considerate neighbor pours coffee, in front of the lone chimney, for deputy sheriffs and fire-fighters.

Firefighters at the Big House fire

Once again, TCCS met adversity and prevailed with the help of its families and surrounding community. The next days and weeks to come would be trying for both the adults and children. Students walked past the ashes of their once Big House and across a newly built stile that now connected TCCS to their neighbor's guest cottage that became the children's temporary sleeping quarters.

Bryan Epps, a 13 year old at the time, describes his feelings after the fire. *"The evening of the night the Big House burned, I had helped a boy move a bed in a room of it. After the fire, I looked at a half-burned and badly scorched banister that had led to the room. I had walked up those stairs with my hand on that banister. The stairs, the room, the bed, the whole Big House just wasn't there! It seemed impossible. Yet, it was so."*

THE CHILDREN'S COUNTRY SCHOOL
Los Gatos, California

February 12, 1945 Volume 1, Number 1

HERE WE ARE AGAIN!

Well, well! Here we are starting the New Year bright and shining with our newspaper, HAPPY TIMES, at the top of the list. It is going to be more than full of interesting happenings at the school. Perhaps you'll laugh at the jokes and little verses, written by the younger members, and their little drawings to go with them. You won't know what to expect from the outstanding events and editorial because everything from a new puppy to an unusual movie will be included.

With almost every story or piece of news there will be a picture that (we hope) will make you feel that you are having the same adventures and enjoy the same good times that we enjoy ourselves.

Eleanore Atkins, Grade 7.

Happy Times special edition for Big House fire

The day after the fire with fire extinguishers left behind on campus

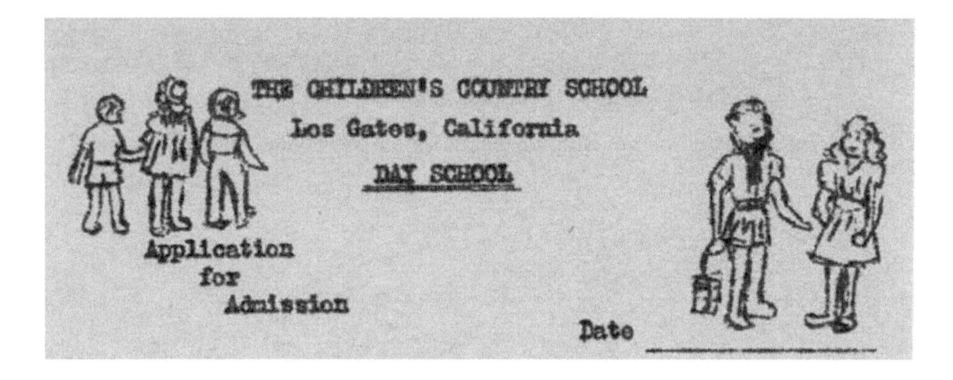

THE CHILDREN'S COUNTRY SCHOOL

Los Gatos, California

DAY SCHOOL

Application
for
Admission

Date ____________

CHAPTER 11

RISING FROM THE ASHES

"We are regaining a happy life again, for there is some exciting news that has gone to the hearts of us."

~Noel Crandell

True to their nature, the founders used the fire as a means for teaching. Such topics as white heat, sparks, cinders, and why did the bricks not burn and metal pipes melt were discussed and researched in science. The school newspaper, Happy Times, had reporters researching how many fire stations and forest ranger stations were located in Santa Clara Valley and how they serviced the Valley. Even humor was injected into the newspaper with the printed joke: Why didn't the bulldozers go to the fire?...because they were sleeping. John Brady sums up the aftermath of the fire from the founders' perspective as simply *"This is part of life...a positive experience."*

The devastating fire to their ten bedroom Big House became a rallying point for an ambitious Building Program. In a letter dated six weeks following the fire, Nathalie explains, *"It forces us to continue our building plans for permanent school buildings which was in the dream stage before January 3rd (night of the fire) and is now taking shape in the hands of architects and engineers...the building program must continue; not for the expansion of the school, but for the growth of the individual."*

The Building Program was explained in detail in the school newspaper, Happy Times, by associate editor and 8th grader, Noel Crandell. Under the title 'What Will We Do About It,' Crandell explains, *"The Big House is gone, yes, but our spirits have not gone with it. TCCS is going to start a project of construction for new buildings. Since there is such a shortage of lumber and it costs so much and we want something that won't burn, we are going to replace it with adobe! We are getting the clay from our own school grounds. The children will take an hour a day to work at making the bricks. We all want to earn money to help with the new buildings and many good plans have been suggested. We think it a very good idea to give everybody who wishes an opportunity to buy a brick that we have made. The money will go to help pay for our buildings. We will engrave their name on the brick they buy and put it into the building. With this in mind and the constructive spirit that is always a part of this school, I am sure we will always go forward rapidly in whatever we might have to do."*

Children making bricks for new adobe building

As ambitious as the children's brick-making plan seemed, in reality it became more a symbolic means by which the children could be involved in the building and planning process. Mary believed that children should *"feel a part of the great earth which holds us all together."* The reality was that bricks were made, but not nearly enough to build an entire building. However, what was accomplished may seem as astonishing as children making bricks from clay.

The founders looked to their school community, as well as to the Los Gatos community for help. The Building Program would be funded by the school's first capital campaign. The goal was to raise $40,000 to build a new Adobe dormitory. The hope was to secure 160 interest-free promissory notes of $25 each. The astonishing fact is that not only did they reach their goal, but it was accomplished in a mere six months. The country was still ravaged by war rationing and yet the surrounding community rallied to the aide of the school.

To fully understand the magnitude of this accomplishment, we must compare this 1946 feat to present-day 2011. Since 1946, inflation has increased 1,137% in the United States. If we apply this factor to the monetary notes submitted in 1946, the following figures would be their equivalent in 2011. In 1946, each $25 note would equate to $284 today. The ultimate goal of raising $40,000 in 1946 would equate to a grand total of $455,000 in 2011. Today's equivalent of $455,000 was raised in a six month period; from a student body 5 times smaller than the school population today; from a Los Gatos town demographic 8 times smaller than today; with a total figure nearly double that of the school's total capital campaign amount raised in 2010. Truly amazing!

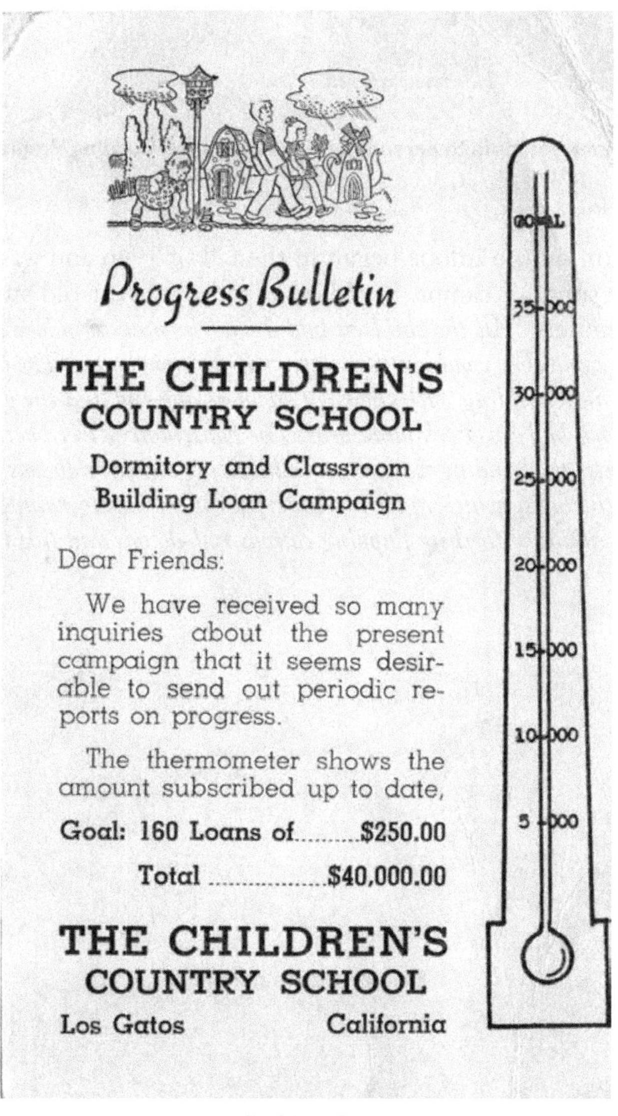

Progress Bulletin

THE CHILDREN'S
COUNTRY SCHOOL

Dormitory and Classroom
Building Loan Campaign

Dear Friends:

We have received so many inquiries about the present campaign that it seems desirable to send out periodic reports on progress.

The thermometer shows the amount subscribed up to date,

Goal: 160 Loans of.........$250.00

Total $40,000.00

THE CHILDREN'S
COUNTRY SCHOOL

Los Gatos California

1946 Building Program

The Children's Country School

Please accept our thanks for your kindness in making the non-interest bearing loan represented by the enclosed notes.

This loan made it possible for us to proceed with our building plans and provide the first wing of a new dormitory for our children.

We are deeply appreciative.

Mary Orem
President
Board of Directors

Thank you note to parents for donating to the Building Program

Construction on the Adobe began in the fall of 1946 and was completed in time for summer camp. Freddie Kulper, a 10 year old student at the time, remembers *"All the children had a part in making adobe bricks on the site. We were told they would be used as part of our new home. The plan consisted of a rectangular building with the boy's dorm at one end and the girl's dorm at the other. Each had six or ten bunk beds. The housemother lived between the two dorms. Because the building was on an incline, a big cement slab was poured along the back of the house which made a wonderful roller skating ramp. It was good to leave the cabins with their flapping canvas roll-downs and live in a nice new building."*

The new adobe dormitory

Education is fluid, active, limitless, a continuous leading out into greater knowledge. It must be experimental—or else it will be too circumspect, limited, stagnant and so cease to be education.

An individual is made up of inherited tendencies, environmental and emotional experiences, his thought about himself in his relation to society—his conception of his place in the universe.

CHAPTER 12

OH BILLY...SHE'S GONE

"Plant my seed in holy ground
In honest soil of simple living
Un-mixed with tawdy adult wills
The artificial love of worldly thinking men
Let my roots search deep the rich and fertile earth
With experience past"

~Mary Orem

Mary Orem in 1946

The Children's Country School had prevailed through a national Depression and World War. Its main classroom and dormitory building had been destroyed by fire and replaced by a new adobe dormitory in a little over a year's time. TCCS was again looking towards the future since becoming a non-profit corporation. Unfortunately, this future would become less clear with the loss of its moral compass and philosophical leader.

In 1946, Mary was diagnosed with cancer. Being a Christian Scientist, she was not privy to medication. She spent her final months resting at the school-owned beach house in Rio Del Mar. One year to the day of being elected President of TCCS, Mary Orem died on January 2, 1947.

Many students do not recall knowing that she was sick and even more astounding that she passed away at the time. John Brady states, "*Since she was Christian Scientist, you didn't refer to someone being sick for it showed weakness of spirit. It was quiet. It was very low key to my young perspective. I remember it was Ann Boge who got us together and we talked about it briefly that she was gone and wasn't coming back. And that was all.*"

Children with Mary Orem

Bill Yabroff describes that day as a young 17 year old. Bill told me that he remembers his mother coming up to him crying and throwing her arms around him sighing, "*Oh, Billy, she's gone.*" Bill didn't even know that she was sick.

Richerd Cancilla continued to board at the school during high school. He adds "*when Mary Orem died it was a big loss for me. I did have a real love for her that I didn't realize until she was gone. It left a hole. That's when I realized how much I thought of her.*"

It is interesting that a woman who took every opportunity to turn a negative situation such as a World War or tragic on-campus fire into a relevant, teachable moment, quietly and with little significance left TCCS. However, her silent departure would be masked by her philosophical writings that she left behind for leading a progressive school.

Mary writes, "*Education must be experimental or else it will be too circumspect, limited, stagnant, and so cease to be education. Activity unharnessed is liable to cause destruction. Activity directed into right channels is sure to make for re-construction. The wide expanses of hills-the simple soil-the inspiring closeness to nature; contact with the soil without which no child's life is complete. Care of the animals, planning for their well-being which is a first step toward thinking outside of self.*"

Mary Orem teaching students

Bill Yabroff escorting Mary Orem to 1946 Graduation ceremony

Mary believed children should have *"opportunity to share with others the physical care and upkeep of their little community-to win a place of responsibility in that community through individual manifestation of his own superior abilities-to learn the great lessons following the experience of failure to do one's share, to come through with a responsibility. Supply experimental opportunities conducive to understanding of problems confronting people in their living together-such as the Village of Friendly Relation- as a first step to an understanding of the problem confronting peoples of the world-the ultimate aim, the 'Peace Tower.' Without the God qualities of honesty, compassion, and obedience to principle, life has no purpose and knowledge could become a tool of destruction."*

Mary, who never even wanted to have her picture taken, once told Nathalie that she never wanted a monument in her honor. What Mary didn't visualize was a school that some 60 years after her death was her monument to every thing that she put into her *"little country school."*

TO SANTA CRUZ
This Way to
The CHILDREN'S
COUNTRY
SCHOOL
Kennedy Road, Route 3, Box 13
Los Gatos, California
The
CHILDRENS
COUNTRY
SCHOOL
KENNEDY

CHAPTER 13

AN IDEA IN ITSELF

"They walked arm and arm occupying the whole width of the street, and taking in every Musketeer that they met, so that in the end it became a triumphal march."

~The Three Musketeers

In 1947, the Children's Country School called an emergency meeting of the Board of Director's following the death of their director, Mary Orem. The last entry of the meeting minutes states, "*To follow the plans and ideals so wonderfully outlined for us, this will be our ever-present guide. We humbly and prayerfully take up the work before us and with God's help we pledge our devotion and energies to tend the growing school, the God-given inspiration of Mary Orem. May we not fail!*"

TCCS would become a day school in 1956. Miss Saki would leave TCCS to become a public school teacher. Her departure and her immense value as a housemother prompted the school to no longer provide boarding for students. Miss Saki would go on to have a successful career as a 1st grade public school teacher and earn the California Teacher of the Year Award in 1967.

Nathalie would become head of school in 1947 following the death of Mary Orem. She would remain head of school through 1967. In 1960, she changed the name of the school to Hillbrook at the request of the junior high school students who felt that the name TCCS was too 'childish.' The new name, Hillbrook, reflects the school campus of hills with a stream or brook running through it. Nathalie's son, Bill Yabroff, would take over for his mother as head of school in 1968. Nathalie would continue to be a member of the Board of Directors into the 1970's. True to her creative spirit, she spent her first night as a resident of Los Gatos Meadows playing piano and leading a sing-along for residents. Nathalie would succumb to cancer in 1978.

December 29, 1947

An emergency meeting was held in order to adjust to the passing of our beloved president, Mary Orem, on December 27th, 1947.

Ann Boge was named president pro-tem and Elizabeth was vice-president, pro-tem.

It was unanimously agreed the Mary Orem, the founder of T.C.C.S. would remain our "leader and director emeritus."

"To follow the plans and ideals so wonderfully outlined for us, this will be our ever-present guide. We humbly and prayerfully

Emergency meeting of the Board of Directors

Miss Saki

'The Hillbrook School'

Country School to change name

Nathalie Wollin

Nathalie Wollin announcing that TCCS becomes Hillbrook School in 1960

Clare Yabroff states, "*She really gave her life to the school you know in the 50's living in the Tower by herself and running the school. I think she was proud of it and believed in it, but she sacrificed a great deal for it.*"

Ann Boge and Elizabeth Glassford would retire from TCCS in the 1960's. Together, they purchased a three apartment complex near Main Street in Los Gatos. Elizabeth would live to be 96 and Ann would live to be 92 years old. Elizabeth was described by Nathalie's grand-daughter as a real character in retirement that always had a wistful demeanor hence her nickname "Cheery." Ann was the antithesis to Elizabeth, as she was both quiet and reserved.

Ann Boge

Elizabeth Glassford

All four women were strong willed and confident, but together, they were effective partners. As you drive down Shannon Road in Los Gatos, nearby you will find side streets with the names of Glassford, Wollin, Orem, and Boge. These four women dedicated their life to The Children's Country School.

Elizabeth writes, "*Children are not to be classified with stocks and bonds and other material, cherished possessions, accumulated over a period of years, and subject to the thermometer of man-made conditions. Let the cave man instinct of intense possession enslave material things, but little children should have the privilege of a free birthright and with their feet in the solid earth of parents security and love grow up into the sunshine and branch out in self-expression and self-reliance.*"

In 1936, Mary's words apply two-fold today; "*Education is fluid, active, limitless, a continuous leading out into greater knowledge. Be sure that the children's growing comes from their own doing; 'Learn by doing.' Give them an environment that offers opportunities for deeper living.*"

Nathalie concludes, "*Everyone has something to express. Here, the way to freedom in self-expression is shown to each child. I feel that to be here and see the development of these children, from the usual unsure and afraid-to-be-laughed-at child that comes to us, to the gracious, free, happy child who gives his best because his desire to give to others is strong enough as to blot out self-consciousness, is a privilege.*

...It didn't belong to anyone. It was an idea in itself. The perfect idea and it needed to go on. And it will go on."

As the twig is bent, the tree will grow.

Nathalie Wollin, Mary Orem, Elizabeth Glassford, Ann Boge

The Village of Friendly Relations in 2011

The CHILDREN'S COUNTRY SCHOOL
Day and Boarding

ENDNOTES

[1] "Famous Quotes by Women From American History: Elizabeth Blackwell." American History Fun-Facts.com. Web. 3 Apr. 2011. <http://www.american-history-fun-facts.com/famous-quotes-by-women.html>.

[2] Ancestry.com, 1900 United States Federal Census Record for Mary E. Orem, Utah.

[3] Press Reference Library (Southwest Edition) *Los Angeles Examiner*, Los Angeles, 1912, pg. 428.

[4] Utah Development Company, Maine: Capitol Stock signed by A.J. Orem, The State of Maine, 1905.

[5] Elsie Jones-Smith, *Theories of Counseling and Psychotherapy* (Thousand Oaks, CA: SAGE Publications, Inc, 2011), Chapter 3.

[6] Novelguide.com, *The 1930's: Overview: Education*, http://www.novelguide.com/a/discover/adec_0001_0004_0/adec_0001_0004_0_01121.html accessed February 2011.

[7] Jane Addams, *Twenty Years at Hull House*. New York: MacMillan, 1912. 227. (founded 1889)

[8] *Wikipedia: Jane Addams*, http://en.wikipedia.org/wiki/Jane_Addams

[9] Maurice Hamington, *The Stanford Encyclopedia of Philosophy*: Progressive Vision, http://plato.stanford.edu/archives/summer 2010/entries/addams-jane/ p7, Summer 2010, accessed March, 2011.

[10] Judith Silva, "Yung See San Fong House," Santa Clara County: California's Historic Silicon Valley, http://www.nps.gov/nr/travel/santaclara/text.htm#yun (Washington, D.C.: U.S. Department of the Interior, 2011).

[11] Patrick Casey, *The Rugby History Society*, http://therugbyhistorysociety.co.uk/mitchellmm.html accessed

[12] "Parker Estate Purchased by Country School," *Los Gatos Times* 11 June, 1936.

[13] Algis Ratnikas, *Timelines of History*, http://timelines.ws/20thcent/1934_1935.HTML accessed

[14] W.H. Wones. *Zephyr Point Conference Grounds Brochure. Zephyr Cove*, NV: Presbyterian Church Synod, California-Nevada. Print.

[15] Cream of Wheat. Advertisement. "TAKE NO CHANCES, MOTHER! When your baby is ready for solid food," *Ladies Home Journal* Mar. 1933. Print.

[16] *Wikipedia: Hendrik Willem van Loon*, http://en.wikipedia.org/wiki/Hendrik_Willem_van_Loon accessed
Additional Endnotes

[17] John S. Baggerly, *Los Gatos Weekly-Times*, 2 Feb. 2002: 1-2.

[18] Edward Rothstein, "Forgive me, father, for I am a lapsed pianist," The New York Times, 15 Jan. 1995. http://www.nytimes.com/1995/01/15/arts/classical-view-forgive-me-father-for-i-am-a-lapsed-pianist.html?src=pm accessed September 22, 2011.

[19] John S. Baggerly, *Los Gatos Times-Observer*, 7 Oct. 1988: 3.

[20] David B. Pearson. *Paul Robeson*. Photograph. Web. 15 July 2011. <http://www.silentladies.com/Robeson/Robeson12.jpg>.

[21] *USO Tour, 1944*. Photograph. *Images of America: Los Gatos. San Francisco*: Arcadia, 2004. 104. Print.

[22] Hadelberg Applegate, "Village of Friendly Relations." Photograph. *Sunset* Sept. 1939: 4.

[23] Dick Sparrer, *Los Gatos Weekly Times*, 11 Aug. 2004: 1.

[24] Los Gatos Civil Defense Council Repository. *WWII Blackout Flyer*, 10 Dec. 1941. Print. Charles Bergtold Collection.

[25] "Children's Country School is Heavily Hit By Big Night Fire," *Los Gatos Times* 5 Jan. 1945.

[26] Alexandre Dumas, *The Three Muskateers.* London: George Routledge and Co., 1853. 71.

[27] "Country School to Change Name," *Los Gatos Times* 1960.

CPSIA information can be obtained at www.ICGtesting.com
Printed in the USA
LVOW01s0243010715

444489LV00022B/251/P